About the Author

Dr Lauren Finka is a feline behaviour and welfare advisor for Battersea Dogs and Cats Home, and a post-doctoral research fellow at Nottingham Trent University. In the course of her PhD she studied personality traits in cats, and has used this to develop a tool called the L-Cat, which assesses the behaviour of cats in rehoming centres in order to improve the rehoming process. Dr Finka has previously worked for several different rehoming centres and is a passionate advocate for feline welfare. She regularly speaks internationally about cat behaviour and welfare and also works with International Cat Care on various welfare-related projects. Dr Finka is also a regular contributor to magazines such as *Your Cat*.

The Cat Personality Test

How well do you really
know your cat?

Dr Lauren Finka

EBURY
PRESS

1 3 5 7 9 10 8 6 4 2

Ebury Press, an imprint of Ebury Publishing
20 Vauxhall Bridge Road
London SW1V 2SA

Ebury Press is part of the Penguin Random House
group of companies whose addresses can be found
at global.penguinrandomhouse.com

Penguin
Random House
UK

First published by Ebury Press in 2019

www.penguin.co.uk

A CIP catalogue record for this book is
available from the British Library

ISBN 9781529105278

Printed and bound in Great Britain by Clays Ltd, Elcograf S.p.A.

MIX
Paper from
responsible sources
FSC® C018179

Penguin Random House is committed
to a sustainable future for our business,
our readers and our planet. This book is
made from Forest Stewardship Council®
certified paper.

This book is dedicated to Barry, a cat with an amazing personality. He was an incredible companion, teacher, research assistant, and loyal napping partner. He will be forever missed.

CONTENTS

INTRODUCTION

The domestic cat: A brief history through time

For about 10,000 years or so, humans have enjoyed the company of cats in one form or another. It's thought that it wasn't until about 4,000 years ago that people first began to see cats as 'pets' rather than just free pest control. Fast forward to today, the domestic cat is now one of the most globally common pets around, in some cases outperforming their canine counterparts in popularity. While we share our hearts and our homes with these beautiful furry creatures, in many ways they still remain a bit of an enigma and it's clear we still have a lot to learn!

What we do know about them is how relatively similar they remain to their closest wild relatives, the African (or Near Eastern to be more precise) wildcat, a species still around today. These similarities extend right from their genes to their appearance and behaviour. This understanding of their origins is very useful in explaining many of the 'whys' and 'hows' of the domestic cat's behaviour today. In a comparatively short space of time, the cat has gone from solitarily roaming the planes of the fertile crescent (an area within the Middle East) to curling up on sofas next to humans throughout the world. While they are certainly a very adaptable species, for an animal whose brain may often still be programmed to think more like an independent wildcat than a loving pet, this giant shift in lifestyle is not without its challenges. What's also very clear is how variable the personality of cats can be. Indeed, domestic cats were potentially one of the first species about which natural historians, such as the great Charles Darwin, began to contemplate the emotional lives of animals and their individual differences. These differences can drastically influence the ways cats perceive the world around them and how they respond. As loving owners, the best service we can do for our cats is to appreciate their origins, their individual differences and how we can use this understanding to better meet their needs.

What's inside?

This book is intended to be a fun, easy-to-use guide filled with plenty of quizzes and expert advice for all cat owners alike. Through the following chapters, you'll learn more about your cat's character, how they're feeling and what they can cope with; why they are the way they are; and what makes them tick. Each section is filled with practical tips and support to help you optimise your relationship with them and, ultimately, ensure they have a good quality of life. The book's contents have been created by a leading cat behaviour scientist, based on up-to-date scientific thinking. While the quizzes are not scientifically validated 'tests' as such, the information and advice provided is based on current best practice and scientific evidence where available. If you're looking for a book to give you more insight into the mind of your precious feline, their individual character and how best to accommodate this, then this one's definitely for you!

SECTION 1:
THE HUMAN'S CAT

In this section

How does your cat feel about you?

How does your cat like to be stroked?

Is your cat ready to live with a baby?

As cat owners, we often form close social bonds with our furry friends that can be very beneficial for both our, and their, wellbeing. However, sometimes it might feel as if the love affair we have with them is a bit one-sided. As a cat enthusiast, you will no doubt have encountered the extremes of the feline character, from being practically addicted to their humans to seeming to be physically allergic to our presence. Due to their aloof, wildcat ancestry, domestic cats aren't necessarily born with a love for humans. Cats need to have the right kind of personality and positive early experiences with us, at the right age, in order to be able to reciprocate our affections. If cats are living as our pets, how friendly and confident they feel around us is often crucial in determining the type of bond we are able to have with them, as well as how comfortable they ultimately are, living closely alongside us. Using the quiz that follows, you can assess how friendly and confident your cat is towards people and what you can do to optimise the relationship you have with them, keeping them as happy as possible.

How does your cat feel about you?

Does your cat prefer you or food?

Get a small handful of your cat's usual dry food, or some treats, and one of their favourite toys. Sit or kneel down a few metres away from your cat and place the treats and toy either side of you, about level with your knees. Use your smoochiest cat voice to call your cat over and offer them your hand (palm facing down). Only stroke them if they decide to rub against you. Observe your cat for 60 seconds. Ideally, repeat the above several times at different times of the day. Each time, alternate where you place the toys and treats so that sometimes they are both to your left or right, but always the same distance away from your cat.

Did your cat:

A. Trot on over, making a beeline for you and your chin tickles

B. Walk over, quickly inspect each item, then give you a few head rubs before moving on to the treats

C. Saunter over, give you a sniff, then eat some treats or start batting at the toy

D. Cautiously approach, grab a mouthful of treats, then scarper

E. Stay where they were and pretend they didn't hear you calling them

What do you need to do to get your cat to approach you?

A. I don't need to do anything – my cat won't leave me alone!

B. Just a little gentle encouragement or call their name

C. I may have to call their name a few times and keep patting my lap, but they will usually come eventually

D. Work pretty hard, usually involving a piece of string or by rattling the treat packet

E. Food, and it must be visible

When you're around your cat, do they (tick each relevant box):

☐ Follow you around, often appearing at your side like a little furry stalker

☐ Approach you with their tail held high, perhaps with a small crook in the end like the top of a big furry question mark

☐ Gently wave their tail from side to side in the air, as if plucking at an invisible harp

☐ Weave around your legs as you stumble about and try not to step on them

☐ Happily converse with you via a combination of meows, purrs and 'chirrups'

☐ Rub against you or objects near to you

☐ Purr like a motorboat

☐ Knead you with their front paws, as if you are a loaf of bread

☐ Have a relaxed facial expression, ears pricked and pointed forwards; it's almost as if they're smiling at you

☐ Generally look relaxed and comfortable in your presence

☐ Lie on their side, showing you their tummy (although you should probably just look rather than touch!)

How many of these signs do you see and how often?

A. Most of them, every day

B. Some of them, most days

C. Some of them, occasionally

D. A few of them, but only when I have food

E. None of them, ever

When you're around your cat, do they (tick each relevant box):

☐ Try to maintain a safe distance between the two of you where possible

☐ Walk or move away if you approach them or get too close

☐ Try to leave the room if you enter it or keep quiet and hope you won't spot where they're hiding

☐ Look away from you if you try to get their attention or call their name

☐ Look directly at you without blinking for periods of time – is this a staring contest?

☐ Look tense, hunched or on edge, all four feet on the ground, tail pressed into their body

☐ Have a tense facial expression, ears either rotated backwards or flattened down to the sides

☐ Generally just seem a bit uncomfortable in your presence

☐ Appear to 'freeze' a little if you touch or stroke them

How many of these signs
do you see and how often?

A. None of them, ever

B. One or two of them, sometimes

C. Some of them, occasionally

D. Some of them, most days

E. Most of them, every day

It's evening, and you're sitting in front of the TV with a nice, soft blanket covering your legs. Does your cat:

A. Jump straight up and plonk themselves on your lap, nuzzling you for strokes

B. Rub themselves against your leg, looking for permission to jump up

C. Come and sit by your side, at some point in the evening

D. Sit vaguely near you but not in reach

E. Studiously ignore you and refuse to come anywhere near you all night (except when you're putting their dinner down)

When people are in the same room as your cat, does your cat:

A. Try to get everyone's attention by any means necessary – humans should know better than to ignore their important feline!

B. Do the rounds every now and then, seeing who gives the best chin tickles

C. Pick the quietest-looking person and stick with them for a bit

D. Try their best to make a speedy exit without anyone touching them (shudders)

E. Remain hidden, in the hope that no one has actually spotted them

If your cat could sleep anywhere in the house, where would it be?

A. On your chest, purring sweet nothings into your ear

B. Somewhere on your bed, until you move around too much and annoy them

C. Somewhere in your room but usually not the bed

D. Somewhere quiet, away from snoring humans

E. As far away from you as possible

When do you give your cat attention or fuss?

A. Every day without fail, at regular intervals – if not I'll get in trouble!

B. Every day, when my cat's in the mood for it

C. Often, but my cat has other priorities too!

D. Only when I manage to get close enough/when they will let me

E. Never: this would likely result in some sort of injury

You've got a few people over for a party and the noise levels are increasing. Is your cat:

A. Totally thrilled about this impromptu networking opportunity

B. Keen to do a quick meet and greet (as long as no one tries to pick them up)

C. Seemingly calm but not in the mood to socialise

D. Quite tense, body hunched and alert

E. Extremely worried; they will be hiding for some time now

How does your cat respond to people they've never met before?

A. They must introduce themselves asap!

B. Inquisitively: usually with a good sniff followed by some friendly cheek rubs

C. They like the humans that crouch down and gently offer their hand for inspection

D. They look wary and will usually keep their distance

E. They will be safely hiding until it's quiet again

How does your cat feel about the humans living in their household (or people that visit you regularly)?

A. They love you all equally – favourites aren't allowed, right?!

B. They prefer whoever gives the best chin strokes or has the tastiest treats

C. They are most comfortable around you because you spend more time with them

D. They are generally terrified, or at least avoidant of, everyone except you

E. They prefer whoever keeps their distance and doesn't try to touch them

Interpret your cat's score

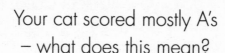

Your cat scored mostly A's – what does this mean?

Congratulations – you likely have a super friendly, confident cat! Your cat is probably into people in a big way – is always around you, interested in what you're doing and keen for attention. While this news may come as no surprise to you, did you ever consider the reasons behind why your cat is more 'doglike' than 'catlike'? The most likely explanation for this is that your cat has a special combination of factors that has shaped his or her personality in this way. For example:

Your cat had the right kind of parents

Research has found that kittens fathered by bold, friendly males are more confident and exploratory at one year of age. Other studies also indicate that if the kitten's mother is calm and relaxed around people, then her kittens will also be less anxious and more keen to interact with people too.

24

Your cat had the right kind of upbringing

Your cat was likely socialised to humans during his or her 'sensitive period' (2–7 weeks of age). Research suggests that this is the most important period in which to positively socialise cats. During this time their brains are considered more 'plastic' and they are more receptive to new experiences and learning. Research shows that kittens that are consistently handled for the duration of their sensitive period are more amenable to handling later in life and quicker to approach people, compared to kittens that are only handled for part, or none, of their sensitive period, even if they receive the same quantity of handling overall. Additionally, studies have shown that the more time kittens are handled each day (up to an hour), the greater the positive impact on their friendliness.

Your cat was likely handled by more than one person during his or her 'sensitive period'. Research suggests that cats that are handled by up to five different people (ideally a mix of both men and women, young and old) are more likely to be comfortable and confident around strangers.

Your cat likely received gentle, positive handling during his or her 'sensitive period'. Research demonstrates that kittens that are handled in a gentle, calm way are more likely to accept and enjoy handling.

Tips and advice

Your cat is likely to enjoy regular interaction with humans – to him or her, you are an important commodity! However, if you have more than one cat, or other pets, ensure you put aside some quality time for each pet each day so that he or she can properly get their attention fix! If your cat wants attention from you but needs to compete with other animals (or even people) in order to get it, this can be frustrating for them and potentially cause conflict and stress. Setting aside some regular, one-on-one time with your cat can help alleviate this problem. Some cats may prefer to interact with us at certain times of the day. If this is the case for your cat, sticking to a daily routine can be beneficial for them. You might also find that this consistency will help to stop your cat from pestering you for attention when you are busy and need to focus on other things (this is particularly handy for those of us that work from home!). For example, if your cat knows that 'fuss time' is roughly always 8–9am and then 2–4pm, he or she may happily go off and do their own thing in between these times. On the other hand, if your cat never quite knows when the attention is coming, they may be more likely to be constantly waiting around, pestering you for it!

While your super friendly, confident cat will probably always be up for some attention from you, each cat will have its own preference for how he or she likes to be stroked and interacted with, so it's important to pay attention to what your cat prefers. If given half a chance, some friendly cats will glue themselves to our laps for most of the day, while others may prefer a 'little and often' approach. The latter may prefer to have a quick stroke, go off and explore for a bit, then come back for another round. Similarly, some cats will enjoy being stroked from top to toe (even in the most divisive of places – the tummy!), while others may prefer that you mainly stick to their chin, cheeks and base of their ears. Getting to know your cat's preferences in this regard is a great way to keep them happy and strengthen the bond you have with them. Take the quiz on pages 36–59 to determine your cat's preferred 'stroking protocol'!

Your cat scored mostly B's and C's – what does this mean?

Congratulations! You have an averagely friendly (but still perfectly wonderful) cat! While your cat is likely to enjoy hanging out with you, he or she will also enjoy having their occasional bit of 'me time'. Fascinatingly, the world that our domestic pet cats occupy couldn't be further from that of their wildcat relatives. These wildcats live primarily solitary lives, avoiding both humans and other cats as much as possible. Respecting the wildcat within your furry friend and ensuring you are careful not to put too much 'social pressure' on them will help to ensure they see you as a source of pleasure rather than stress. Just like with 'A' cats, working out the way your cat prefers to interact with you is also super important.

Tips and advice

While, in the eyes of your cat, you are still likely to be an important resource to them, your cat will probably also benefit from a range of other types of entertainment, in addition to the cat cuddles you provide. These may include things such as interactive toys (i.e. a feathered wand or fishing-rod type toy, operated by you), interactive puzzle feeders and the opportunity to explore outside the house, in an enriched, cat-friendly space. Your cat will also benefit from having some quiet places around the house where he or she can go and relax, undisturbed. This is a really important strategy for your cat so that they can avoid becoming overwhelmed when there's too much going on around them – remember, their solitary relatives are more into peace and quiet than busy social gatherings! Ensure you are aware of your cat's preferences for handling. For example, does he or she prefer full body strokes or just a brief tickle around the chin or cheeks? Does your cat enjoy one or two intensive fussing sessions per day or lots of brief little strokes throughout the day? Take the quiz on pages 36–59 to determine how your cat likes being stroked best.

Your cat scored mostly D's and E's – what does this mean?

At heart, your cat is probably a lot more wild than pet, enjoying their own company a lot more than that of people. It's very likely that, in stark contrast to the super friendly, confident cat, your cat missed out on some of the vital ingredients necessary to create a well-rounded, sociable individual. For example:

Your cat's parents were also not that keen on people

One (or both) of your cat's parents may have been timid and unfriendly towards people. If your cat was the consequence of an unplanned litter, it could be that he or she had feral or free-living (i.e. stray) parents rather than those of a typical pet cat. Many free-living cats will merely tolerate, or completely avoid, people and so the DNA they then pass along to their offspring will usually encourage these behaviours too.

Your cat didn't have the right early experiences

Your cat likely missed out on sufficient socialisation and handling during their 'sensitive period' (2–7 weeks of age).

Cats born to feral or free-living mothers will usually fall into this category: they will often have been captured and brought into a rehoming facility post seven weeks of age; sometimes they may even have been adults when caught. Alternatively, a free-living mother cat may have been brought into a rehoming facility either while pregnant or with young kittens, which she was still feeding. If she was very anxious and stressed in this environment, she will likely have passed on this stress and anxiety to her kittens, who would also begin to associate people with negative experiences. This learning can be very difficult (and stressful for the cat) to undo. These kittens may also have been harder to socialise, given that the mother cat was unlikely to let people near them easily. While it can seem appealing to try to tame or 'bring around' a cat or kitten, if it is already very frightened or wary of people, this process can be very stressful for the cat and you will often be less successful than if you'd social-ised the cat at the appropriate time. Such cats may be much happier being released to a safe outdoor environment (after being neutered, of course) where they can live out their days without much contact from humans, just as their wild rela-tives would choose.

Your cat may have had friendly parents or have been socialised at the right time, but this socialisation may not have been sufficient for your cat to learn that people gener-ally represent something positive. For example, your cat may have only been handled by one person or for too short a time period each day. Alternatively, your cat's early experiences with people may have been predominantly negative or involved some rough handling.

Your cat might be feeling stressed or unwell

It's also possible that your cat's unfriendly, unconfident behaviour could be the result of an underlying medical condition that is causing him or her to feel unwell or in pain. Research shows that chronic pain and illness can greatly alter the behaviour of animals, particularly how they perceive their environment and how they interact with others. Alternatively, your cat could be experiencing stress that is caused by some element of their environment. A stressed cat can also appear less friendly and less keen to interact with people than a relaxed comfortable one.

Tips and advice

Your cat is likely to find the daily hustle and bustle within a typical household a lot to contend with. He or she may also find the affections of people quite daunting, especially those from unfamiliar faces. In this case, the best and kindest way to help your cat to have a good quality of life is to allow them to be as independent and solitary as they choose. In this regard, it may even help to see your cat as being more like their wildcat relatives than a typical pet. Alternatively, you could think of your cat as an expensive lodger that just comes and goes as he or she pleases, receiving free food and accommodation with no expectations to love you back in return. The personality of an adult cat is pretty much fixed, so attempts to get your cat to see you as anything other than a glorified tin opener at this point is pretty futile.

There's a lot you can still do for your cat, though, to make sure they are as happy as possible living alongside you. Your cat is going to prioritise their safety, security and being able to access all of his or her important resources (i.e. food, water, beds, hiding places, litter trays, high-up places) without being disturbed in the process. Your cat will also appreciate having lots of places to rest and also to explore away from people; giving him or her constant access to a large, cat-friendly garden is ideal in this regard. Your cat may even prefer to sleep outdoors so providing a source of shelter and food outside could be perfect. Ultimately, if you get the impression that your cat would be happier living more like their relatives, far away from humans, this may be the best thing for them. Relocating your cat to a quiet, rural area with a safe, warm shelter and a regular food source may be just what they've always dreamed of.

If your cat's avoidant, unfriendly behaviour is a relatively new thing (for example, if they were previously friendly and confident around people), a trip to the vets is always recommended, followed up with a consultation with a suitably qualified cat behaviour counsellor if necessary.

Science corner

Are pedigree cats friendlier?

A study conducted by Dr Finka and colleagues in 2019, looking at cats' behaviour towards humans, found a potential link between the personality of a cat and whether they were a pedigree or not. Compared to domestic short-haired cats, pedigree and pedigree crosses were more likely to score higher in their levels of friendliness and confidence towards their owners and lower for aloofness, fearfulness and handling intolerance. This may be due to the fact that, in general, non-pedigree cats are potentially more likely to be the result of unplanned litters, meaning that at least one of their parents may have been a feral or free-living cat rather than a pet. In contrast, when sourced from a responsible breeder, pedigree cats may be more likely to be bred from two 'friendly' cat parents, with this 'friendly' DNA being passed down to their offspring. Such kittens may also be more likely to be well-handled and socialised to humans during their sensitive period (2–7 weeks of age) before being rehomed.

Are some pedigree breeds friendlier than others?

Other research looking at variations in the behaviour across pedigree cats found several differences among breeds.

A large study of Finnish cats, conducted by Dr Salonen and colleagues in 2019, found that owners of British Shorthaired cats rated their cats as being more aloof but less aggressive towards people, compared to owners of other breeds. In contrast, Korats were least likely to be rated as aloof, and Burmese cats least shy towards strangers, while Russian Blues were rated as the shyest towards both strangers as well as novel objects. Turkish Vans were most likely to be rated as behaving aggressively towards humans as well as other cats. Cornish Rex, Korat and Bengal cats were perceived by their owners as most active, while British Shorthaired cats were considered the least. Finally, owners of Oriental and Persian cats were more likely to indicate their cat displayed a behaviour problem, and Burmese and Oriental cats more likely to over-groom.

While these results are certainly interesting, merely obtaining a pedigree rather than a moggy, or choosing a specific breed of cat, is definitely no guarantee that he or she will have a certain personality type. When it comes to the behaviour of cats, their social experiences with humans, as well as the type of environment they are kept in, are particularly important to focus on. Additionally, cats used for breeding purposes are not always kept in environments that are good for their wellbeing. Some pedigree breeds (Exotics, Persians, Munchkins and Scottish Folds for example) are also linked with chronic health issues, such as breathing problems and degenerative joint disease.

Do cats mirror our own personalities?

The study conducted by Dr Finka also found a link between the cat's personality and that of its owner. Owners that were more neurotic were found to have cats that scored higher for anxiety and fear, as well as handling intolerance. On the other hand, owners that were more extroverted, open and conscientious owned cats that scored higher for friendliness and confidence. Additionally, owners that were more agreeable, open and conscientious had cats that were more tolerant to handling, and less aloof and avoidant. Finally, owners that were more conscientious had cats that were less fearful and anxious. These results suggest that, just like with parents and their children, cats can be affected by our personalities and the type of 'parenting' we expose them to.

How does your cat like to be stroked?

Many cats clearly enjoy being fussed, tickled and caressed to their heart's desire. However, as most cat-stroking enthusiasts will have discovered, this doesn't apply to them all! As humans, we are generally drawn to small, cute furry animals and our instincts are often to cuddle and caress them as much as possible. However, unlike the domestic dog, the closest wild relative of the domestic cat, the African wildcat, is mostly solitary and decidedly non-tactile or 'un-cuddly'. What this means is that domestic cats aren't necessarily born ready to enjoy being stroked or touched a lot; instead, they need the right kind of personality and early experiences to help them to like it – and some cats will end up liking it much more than others. Some cats will be very clear of their dislike of your petting, while other cats may quietly put up with it. Interestingly, while you might think that the cat that protests the loudest suffers the most, studies suggests that, in some cases, it's the cats that are suffering in silence (i.e. just tolerating it) that are the more stressed.

So, what can influence a cat's preference for being stroked and how can we assess this? Each cat is an individual so if they like to be stroked (and how) will depend on several factors, including:

🐾 *Their personality – the more friendly and confident the cat, the more likely they are to enjoy being touched*

🐾 *Individual differences – some cats might be more sensitive on different parts of their body (like their tummy, for example) or feel more pleasure in certain areas (some cats may really enjoy their face and head being touched and nowhere else)*

🐾 *Their early experiences – the more gentle and positive handling the cat received during kittenhood (and thereafter) the better*

When it comes to being stroked, there's a big difference between putting up with it and actually liking it! Because we want our furry friends to enjoy their fussing session as much as we do, it's helpful for us to be able to find out what our cat really prefers. The following tests have been created to help you understand your cat's likes and dislikes. By the end of this quiz, you'll be able to turn cat-stroking into an art form.

How keen is your cat to interact with you?

Sit or kneel down about a metre away from your cat. If you need to, politely get their attention (make a few of your usual smoochy cat noises, for example). Gently offer your hand (palm facing down) towards your cat. Pause with your hand in this position for 20 seconds and allow your cat to choose whether they make contact. Observe your cat. You can say the odd word of encouragement if it helps. Ideally, repeat the above several times at different times of the day.

Did your cat:

~~~~~~

A. Start smooching, rubbing and climbing all over you before you even managed a 'Here, Tiddles!'

B. Give you a good amount of cat-on-human action, but with little pauses in between – 20 seconds of contact is actually quite a lot!

C. Take their time but eventually come over, humour you with a half-hearted sniff or cheek rub, then start looking for the treat packet

D. Give a brief glance in your direction then pretend to carry on with whatever it was they were doing before you decided to disturb them with this silly test

E. Give you the evils before getting out of there as quickly as possible – how could you forget the 2m boundary rule?!

F. Or: You have no idea because you couldn't even locate him/her; they are probably hiding from you

On which parts of your cat's body do they usually enjoy being stroked or tickled?

A. Pretty much every one of these places, in particular 1–2 – always, without fail!

B. Always 1, usually 2 and sometimes 3–6

C. Usually 1, although they might *tolerate* some other areas being touched

D. Occasionally 1 but only if there's likely to be food involved and you'd better get it over with fast!

E. None of them ever

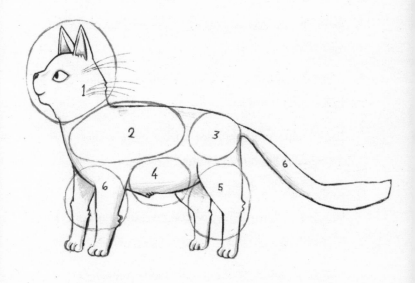

Stroke your cat in the way you usually would for about five seconds, then stop. Observe what your cat does next.

Did your cat:

A. Instantly rub you or paw at you – why on earth did you stop, human?!

B. Calmly turn to look in your direction and maybe lean in for a bit more

C. Look comfortable, but not ask for more – short and sweet suits them juuust fine!

D. Only allow you about two seconds before they scarper and/or deliver a 'continue at your peril' sort of warning

E. Not applicable: stroking your cat is not something that ends well for either of you

When you stroke your cat, do you ever notice them do any of the following? (tick each relevant box)

☐ Moving or walking away from you as if you're contagious or something

☐ They no longer seem to have any limbs (they are all safely tucked away from your horrible, clammy hands)

☐ Remaining relatively passive during the whole process, in the hope that this helps it to be over quicker

☐ Blinking, shaking their head or body or licking their nose; brain reset is being attempted

☐ Suddenly deciding they are extremely dirty and launching into a frantic grooming session

☐ Skin twitching or rippling as if someone just walked over their grave

☐ Tail taking on the appearance of an angry snake, swishing furiously from side to side or thumping up and down

☐ Suddenly going a bit still, doing their best statue impression

☐ Ears flattening downwards or rotating towards the back of their head

☐ Sharply turning their head to face you or your hand, accompanied by a death stare

☐ Biting or swiping at you, or bopping you with their paw – take that, annoying human!

☐ Hissing, growling or emitting an unpleasant sort of groaning noise – pay attention, or you'll get what's coming to you!

How often do you see any of these signs?

A. Never! We are both equal fans of cuddle time

B. Occasionally, but usually only when I push things too far or try to touch the 'forbidden' areas

C. Quite often: it's almost as if my cat's trying to tell me something …

D. Pretty much every time without fail – OK, maybe it's time to change tactics a bit

E. Stroking would involve physical contact and we don't do that!

When you stroke your cat, do you ever notice them do any of the following? (tick each relevant box)

☐ Rubbing themselves all over you as if it's been a year since they last saw you

☐ Sticking themselves to you like a cat-shaped magnet

☐ Purring like a motorboat

☐ Kneading you with their front paws as if you are a loaf of bread

☐ Holding their tail upright, standing to attention; it may also have a small crook in the end like a big furry question mark

☐ Gently waving their tail from side to side in the air, as if plucking at an invisible harp

☐ A relaxed facial expression, ears pricked and pointed forwards; it's almost as if they're smiling at you

☐ Generally looking relaxed and comfortable – it's nice having a personal masseuse!

☐ Falling asleep at some point – all this loving is exhausting!

☐ Giving you a gentle nudge with their cheek to let you know your stroking speed needs increasing

☐ Following you around until they've had enough – I say when it's over, human!

How often do you see any of these signs?

A. Absolutely always

B. Pretty much every time, except when I know I'm being a bit too full on with the stroking

C. Some of the time – why do I often get the feeling my cat has something better to do?!

D. Occasionally, but I get the impression their heart isn't really in it

E. Again, we don't partake in this activity

Your cat's booked in for a visit to your new 'feline wellness centre'. What would they be likely to request?

Treatment – would they opt for:

A. A full body massage

B. An Indian head massage

C. A light facial

D. Any treatment where you don't actually need to touch them (such as Reiki)

E. Any treatment where you just leave them alone in a dark room for an hour

Intensity – are they likely to go in for:

A. An intense deep-tissue massage

B. A medium-pressure Swedish massage

C. A delicate skin cleansing

D. They will allow you merely to send them some positive vibes from a distance

E. Please don't even look in their direction

Duration – would they prefer:

A. Several consecutive treatments, starting with a relaxing facial, then moving on to a full body massage and a touch of spiritual cleansing at the end

B. A regular treatment

C. A mini taster-session

D. To cancel

E. To give their voucher to Fred next door (and they don't even like Fred that much)

Frequency – when will you see them next?

A. When they offer to employ you as their personal masseuse

B. They would prefer set, regular appointments, preferably several times a day

C. They are more of an occasional 'day pass' kind of cat

D. They might drop in again if they feel like it, but don't want to commit to anything right now

E. Never: this was likely the worst experience of their life and they left feeling more stressed than ever

Interpret your cat's score

Your cat scored mostly A's
– what does this mean?

You don't need a quiz to tell you that you're the proud parent of a total love bug. Your cat is one of those rare specimens that totally defies its aloof, un-cuddly ancestry. Keep doing what you're doing because it seems to be working.

Your cat scored mostly B's
– what does this mean?

Your cat likely gets a lot of pleasure out of stroking sessions with you, although they probably have a preferred 'stroking protocol' that they would like you to adhere to. Each cat is an individual, so getting a good sense of your cat's specific preferences will help to make each session as enjoyable as possible for you both.

Tips and advice

Don't forget that even cuddle addicts may feel like a day off every now and then, so be mindful of some of the signs that might suggest your cat would prefer a bit of 'me time'. They may be too polite or patient to tell you in an obvious way, so look out for some of the following tells:

- 🐾 *You offer them your hand and they decide not to reciprocate with the usual cheek rubs*

- 🐾 *They politely turn their head to face away from you*

- 🐾 *They don't rub you as enthusiastically as usual*

- 🐾 *They go a little bit still or quiet during your stroking session*

- 🐾 *They stay around for a bit, then decide it's time to politely excuse themselves*

Additionally, think about where, when, how much, how long for and how often your cat likes being stroked. Use your answers from the above quiz to help you better understand your cat's specific stroking preferences.

Your cat scored mostly C's – what does this mean?

While this certainly doesn't mean your cat hates you, for him or her to be able to enjoy physical contact with you, they really need to feel as though they have complete choice and control. Some cats are also just more particular about the where, when and how of being touched (just like us basically). It's likely that either your cat is a lot less into strokes than you are or that you're just not doing it right! But don't dismay: we've designed a unique C.A.T. stroking algorithm to ensure future success when interacting with your cat. While it might mean you end up stroking your cat a little differently to usual, this special algorithm will go a long way to make this a much more positive experience for your cat.

Tips and advice

Introducing the C.A.T. stroking algorithm. Use this each time you interact with your cat:

Choice and control

🐾 *Did I let my cat **choose** whether he or she wanted to be touched?*

🐾 *Am I allowing my cat **control** over when the stroking ends?*

The best way to achieve the above is to allow your cat to make the first move; gently offer your hand towards your cat and allow them to decide whether to rub against you or not. If they don't, this is probably because they're just not in the mood (and that's OK!). Never restrain your cat or pick them up when stroking them and always stop or allow them to saunter off when they've had a sufficient amount. If your cat does make contact, you can progress on to the next stage ...

Am I paying attention?

🐾 ***Am I looking** out for any signs that my cat is enjoying what I'm doing or, equally, is feeling uncomfortable? (See the lists of behaviours mentioned in the quiz above)*

While stroking your cat, paying attention to their behaviour and body language will help you to become a total cat-stroking expert. You'll be able to tell what they are and aren't into.

Touch

🐾 *Am I focusing on the areas my cat **prefers being touched**?*

🐾 *Am I checking to see if my cat wants me to **keep touching** them or not?*

The 'safest' place to touch most cats is area 1 on the cat diagram (see page 41), specifically under their chin, the sides of their cheeks and at the base of their ears. These areas all contain special skin glands which your cat uses to deposit their scent onto things by rubbing up against them. These places are therefore likely to be less sensitive than other regions of your cat's body (such as the tummy, for example) and, for most friendly cats, may feel quite nice when stroked. In general, try to avoid areas 3–6 on your cat. Aim to keep stroking brief; you can try the 'three-second rule' whereby you pause stroking every three seconds and only continue if your cat actively asks you for more (by rubbing up against you, for example).

Your cat may also enjoy engaging in a range of non-stroking activities. These could include:

🐾 *Interactive play, using a fishing-rod pole or a feathered wand. This is a great way to keep your cat positively entertained and also allows them to let off some of their predatory steam (at a safe distance from your hands and feet!).*

🐾 *Simply letting your cat hang out near to you or on your lap (without stroking them). Many cats will enjoy being physically close to you without too much fur-on-skin action.*

:paw: *Some basic training, such as teaching your cat to come to you when called , a 'sit' or 'paw'. This works particularly well for confident, food-motivated cats.*

Your cat scored mostly D's and E's – what does this mean?

Your cat is certainly displaying all the classic signs of wanting to steer clear of any of that stroking business. Why this is the case may vary with each cat, but what's really important is to respect that this is the cat's choice and not to push things. Remember that, as humans, we are a sociable and tactile (or touchy-feely) species. This is in stark contrast to the domestic cat's close relatives, which basically try to avoid social gatherings at all costs.

Tips and advice

If you want to interact with and touch your cat, you should certainly implement the C.A.T. algorithm (see pages 53–55). The chances are you won't progress much further than receiving the briefest of sniffs or cheek rubs from your cat, but it may simply be better (and kinder) for both your sakes to accept that your cat simply doesn't like being stroked much at all and that this is probably just part of their personality. It may be that your cat wasn't handled sufficiently, or in the right way, during their sensitive period (at 2–7 weeks of age). It's also possible that years of your cat being handled in a way that he or she doesn't like have simply taken their toll; now they would rather just avoid the situation altogether. If this is the case, you may find that strict adherence to the algorithm over a decent period of time will have more promising results than anticipated!

If your cat used to really like being touched but doesn't seem to any more or you've noticed that he or she has recently started to avoid being stroked, this could be a sign that they are physically unwell, stressed or in pain. In this case, a trip to the vets is always recommended.

Science corner

Why do we find cats cute?

Famous Austrian ethologist Konrad Lorenz was one of the first to try to understand the concept of 'cuteness' and why humans are drawn to facial features that have an 'infantile' appearance. He proposed that humans might be 'biologically programmed' to find big eyes, a large, rounded head, shorter nose and less protruding chin appealing. He suggested that these 'infantile' features may trigger more nurturing or protective feelings in us which, in turn, motivate us to care for babies, young children and perhaps also animals. He termed this concept the 'baby schema'. Interestingly, cats (especially kittens) share many of these attractive baby-like features and research suggests their 'cute' faces might have a similar effect on us.

This may be one of the reasons why some of us find cats with extreme baby-like features particularly cute (for example, Exotic cat breeds and modern Persians, which have very flat, rounded faces and large eyes). These breeds have seen a rise in popularity over the last few decades. However, recent research suggests that such cats may suffer from a range of health problems, in particular breathing difficulties. It's therefore important to ensure that our preferences for cuteness don't come at the expense of our cat's health and wellbeing.

Why do cats rub up against us?
What does it mean?

The domestic cat's wild relatives use parts of their bodies to rub up against prominent things within their environment. They do this to spread their scent, using their specially developed skin glands. These scents contain various chemical messages and pheromones which can be detected by, and used to communicate with, other cats. These messages may be saying things such as 'I live here', 'I was here recently', 'this belongs to me' or 'I'm ready to mate'. Very similar strategies can be observed in our pet cats; they will rub particular parts of their bodies against furniture, new objects in the house, the back door, the garden fence (and, yes – even us), in order to deposit these messages. Our cats are likely doing so to communicate the same kinds of information as their relatives. Cats can also use this rubbing in a more social way and it's thought this might be to create a 'communal scent' by mixing their smell with ours and/or other animals' in the household. They may also rub against us to encourage us to give them attention or feed them. What's important is to be aware that this behaviour may not always mean the same thing and not every cat that rubs against us is necessarily asking us to pick them up or stroke them.

Is your cat ready to live with a baby?

One of the biggest changes in your cat's life may be the arrival of a new baby. While many cats will be thrilled with the addition of a new, non-furry sibling, not all cats will necessarily share this positive outlook. Some cats will require strategic support so that they are able to embrace the small, bald creature that cries a lot and smells funny. Indeed, this is a time where there can be a lot of upheaval for your cat. They may experience changes to their usual routine, get less attention from you than they'd like or perhaps no longer have access to certain parts of the house (such as the baby's room). In addition, there will be lots of new sights, sounds and smells to get used to.

A cat's personality will be very important in determining how well they deal with this situation. Some cats may see this as no biggie, carrying on with life as usual, while others might go into a total meltdown. How you manage your cat and their environment during this time will also go a long way in determining how well he or she is able to cope. It's always better to prevent a stressful situation from happening than to try to fix one that's already occurred.

The following quiz has been designed to help you to gauge where your cat is likely to sit on the 'baby appreciation spectrum', and also provide some tips and advice to help things go as smoothly as possible.

Young children are visiting and they want to interact with your cat. Is your cat:

A. Ready and willing, as long as there's no tail grabbing!

B. Willing to tolerate a bit of stroking, as long as the children are being supervised by a responsible adult

C. Willing to sit near the children, as long as they look but don't touch

D. Plotting ways to get them to leave as soon as possible

E. Already hiding somewhere they will never think to look

Your friends come to visit with their new baby. Where is your cat?

A. Poking their head into the pram, trying to be the first to catch a glimpse

B. Sniffing and rubbing their little furry face on any objects associated with the baby

C. Calmly observing from a slight distance

D. Looking a little agitated and ready to scarper if necessary

E. As far away from everything, and everyone, as possible

Your friend's children stay the night
and it's their crazy hour before bedtime.
There are tantrums and toys being thrown
about. What does your cat do?

A. Attempt to console them by offering a friendly
   head rub

B. Try to help by being as cute as possible to distract
   them

C. Look calmly at the loud, angry little humans but keep
   their distance

D. Get a bit disgruntled by this disruption and scarper

E. They're already hiding and won't be coming out until
   the little devils leave

It's the day of your baby shower and there are lots of people, noise and new gifts around the house. Is your cat:

A. In the middle of all the action, sniffing and rubbing their furry little face over everything – these gifts are all for me, right?

B. Happy about the extra attention but glad this is a one-off event

C. Not a fan of all the noise but pleased with the extra bits of paper and string they get to play with

D. Out of sight, but hoping they will at least get a new cardboard box out of all this

E. Hoping you decide not to have any more kids

You're watching a film with your cat and there's a scene where a baby is crying loudly. Does your cat:

A. Show no interest at all but ask for more popcorn to bat about

B. Briefly look towards the TV, then switch back to snooze mode

C. Become a little tense, raise their head and rotate their ears back slightly – they wish you had better taste in films

D. Quickly disappear into another room to get some peace and quiet

E. It's hard to watch a film together when your cat doesn't want to be in the same room as you

You're super busy, turning the spare
room into a nursery, and you realise
you've neglected your cat a bit.
How do they respond?

A. Like it's totally cool – they know you've been busy,
although they're hopeful that you'll eventually have
some time to squeeze them in for a cuddle session

B. They're not overly keen on this sudden lack of
attention, but they have other stuff they can get on
with until you remember them

C. They are pretty peeved about the whole thing – cats
should come first, not babies!

D. As if they are suffering from the most intense
withdrawal symptoms imaginable

E. Like it's totally cool – they don't like spending time
with you anyway

Interpret your cat's score

Your cat scored mostly A's and B's – what does this mean?

All signs look promising! Your cat is probably the type to take the arrival of their new human sibling well within their stride. They may enjoy, or at least cope very well with, all the new changes associated with your baby's presence. However, each situation is different and it can be very hard to predict exactly how your cat will respond when b-day (baby day) is finally upon them. What's also important is the way that both cat and baby are managed together longer-term. For some cats, the point at which your bundle of joy becomes mobile and wants to grab everything in sight can be a total game changer. Now your young child will start to seem a lot less predictable to your cat, and potentially harder for him or her to avoid. Some cats may also cope better than others as they come to terms with the fact that they are no longer the only small, cute thing in the room.

For all these reasons, and more, what was once a harmonious household can rapidly become hellish. No need to panic, though – implementing some basic strategies can really help to ensure that everyone stays safe and happy!

It's always better to be overly prepared and do more than you may need to than to end up with a stressed-out cat or a scratched child! See further down for advice on the best way to maintain cat and baby harmony.

Your cat scored mostly C's – what does this mean?

Your cat is probably going to find things a bit tricky when the little one finally arrives. They are likely to be super grateful for a bit of support from you to help them cope. This support will also be important through the child's toddler years when furry tails become the most exciting thing for them to grab and pull. The more advance preparation you can do, the easier it will be for your cat to adjust. The more effort you invest in managing cat and toddler as they grow up together, the more likely they are to become friends rather than foes.

Your cat scored mostly D's and E's – what does this mean?

Your cat is unlikely to cope well with all the changes and commotion associated with the arrival of a new baby. They may suddenly feel as if their life has been turned upside down. They may also find an enthusiastic, playful toddler particularly tough to deal with. However, implementing the following advice and techniques will ensure you are doing as much as you can to help your cat feel at ease. Above all else, you should focus on making sure your cat feels safe and that things are still relatively predictable for them. If this is achieved, it will certainly go a long way in helping them feel more comfortable and in control. They will especially appreciate having as much independence as possible: places where they can eat, sleep, rest and toilet undisturbed and (when the little one becomes mobile) access to child-free areas of the house.

Tips and advice for all cats

Advance preparation is key

The best way to prepare is to think about all the things that are likely to change once the baby arrives and gradually get your cat used to them all in advance, creating a gentle transitionary period for them. That way, by the time the baby actually arrives, the only new thing for your cat to adjust to will be the baby itself.

Things that are likely to change include:

🐾 *The person who feeds your cat, where your cat is fed and when*

🐾 *How much attention and play time your cat gets, when and who from*

🐾 *Where your cat's resources are located (for example, their food and water bowls, litter trays, beds, hiding places, scratching posts and toys)*

🐾 *Parts of the house that your cat will no longer have access to*

Ways you can help your furry one to acclimatise:

🐾 *You can try to get your cat used to the various crying, giggling and squealing sounds your baby will emit in advance too. When your cat is relaxed and near to you, you can play recordings of these sounds. Make sure you do this very quietly at first. If your cat appears comfortable, start to gently increase the volume. Make sure to provide your cat with some of their favourite treats to distract and reward them while this is going on.*

🐾 *Try to gradually introduce your cat to various baby paraphernalia (for example, the cot, toys and pushchair) so that by the time the baby arrives, these items are already very familiar – or even boring!.*

🐾 *Each time you introduce a new object into the house, place it in a 'neutral' area (for example, not directly near your cat's resources). Leave some treats on or around the new item, then let your cat explore it in their own time.*

🐾 *If there are items intended for the baby that you don't want your cat to sit or sleep on (such as a cot or pushchair) then it's a good idea to place these out of reach or to cover them with something so that your cat cannot easily jump onto them.*

🐾 *When you bring your baby home, simply let the cat decide when he or she is ready to meet the child. Before their first meeting, it's a great idea to take a small item that has your baby's smell on it and allow your cat to sniff it, along with some treats.*

🐾 *For the safety of both parties, it's a very good idea to not leave the baby and cat together unattended.*

🐾 *Especially in the beginning, you might find you have a lot less time for your cat than they're used to. This loss of attention may be felt the greatest by super friendly love bugs (see quiz on pages 6–35). If this is the case, make sure to leave a little quality time aside for your cat each day, with no other distractions if you can.*

🐾 *You can also make sure they have plenty of other things to keep themselves occupied with when you're not available (see advice on pages 167–70 for ideas).*

🐾 *After the baby arrives, try to keep things as predictable as possible and ensure your cat has lots of quiet, safe spaces where they can go if things get a bit much for them. For more advice on how to do this, see the advice on pages 243–5.*

As your child becomes mobile

🐾 *Providing your cat with lots of places they can sleep, rest and spy on everyone, out of reach of your child, is ideal. A large cat tree, shelves or the tops of cupboards with a cat blanket on are all great ideas. The more of these you can distribute in different places around the home, the more your cat will feel like they just got a posh hotel upgrade.*

🐾 *Installing baby gates is also a great way to put a barrier between your child's inquisitive hands and the cat's food, water and litter trays. This will not only help your cat to be able to eat and toilet in peace, but also ensure your child isn't eating stuff they really shouldn't be.*

🐾 *Alternatively, if space is tight, you might want to start feeding your cat in an elevated location (such as a counter top or shelf they can easily reach).*

Cat–child interactions

🐾 *Even the most patient and good-natured of cats are likely to take issue with noisy, unpredictable toddlers making a beeline for them, grabbing handfuls of fur in the process. It's therefore super important that children learn from the very beginning how to safely and respectfully interact with their furry siblings.*

🐾 *The more calm, gentle and careful the child is around the cat, the more comfortable and less likely the cat is to bite or scratch them.*

🐾 *It's a brilliant idea initially to teach your child how to stroke your cat on a plush cat toy, before moving on to the real thing. This way if anything gets grabbed or pulled too much, your cat won't be paying the price! When your child gets the hang of it, they can then move on to the real thing.*

🐾 *As long as your cat is generally comfortable with being stroked, encourage your child to focus on the areas around your cat's chin, cheeks and just in front of their ears. When they are old enough, you can also start to teach them about your cat's specific 'stroking protocol' (see quiz on pages 36–59).*

✿ *If your cat doesn't really like being stroked, you can teach your child to throw treats for the cat to chase after or play with the cat using a long fishing-rod toy (but NEVER hands or feet!). There are actually lots of ways the two can be friends without the need for excessive physical contact! .*

✿ *Unless your cat seems super comfortable with it, make sure your child avoids picking your cat up. Most cats will shudder at the thought of being unceremoniously heaved about by a small, sticky child.*

How can you tell if your cat is coping well, living with their new human sibling?

To know if your cat is adjusting well to living with a child or baby, you should expect to see:

✿ *No obvious changes to their normal routines and behaviour patterns*

✿ *Your cat continuing to eat, drink, sleep, groom and use their litter tray (where relevant) as usual*

Your cat appearing relaxed and comfortable around the home, including when they are in the proximity of your child

How to tell if your cat isn't coping so well

Despite all your heroic efforts to make things as nice as possible for your cat, some may still struggle to cope. If you're worried this might be the case, take the quiz on pages 181–222 to determine how well your cat's faring and which signs you should be looking out for.

What can you do next?

If you think your cat seems unhappy, it may be a very good idea to seek support from a suitably qualified cat behaviour counsellor. Although, if the situation necessitates it, sometimes the kindest thing is to find a quieter, more stable home for your cat to go to.

Science corner

Do cats communicate with us like babies do?

A fascinating study in 2009 by Dr McComb and colleagues examined the quality of cats' purrs in different situations when around humans. They found that the type of purrs cats make varies, depending on whether the cat is hungry and wants feeding or is relaxed and content. These purrs also have different effects on people who listen to them, with the 'hungry' purrs sounding less pleasant and more urgent than the 'relaxed' purrs. The study also found that the 'hungry purr' contains an extra 'meow' sound within it, which has similar qualities to the cries made by human babies. They found that it is this cry sound that makes the purr seem more urgent. The researchers concluded that cats are potentially producing these special purrs in order to encourage us to want to care for them, tapping into our innate care-giving systems, which usually respond to the cries of human infants. Basically, when we hear these types of purrs, our cats might be subtly manipulating us into feeding them!

SECTION 2:
THE CAT'S CAT

In this section

*Friends or foes – what kind of
relationship do your cats have?*

How comfortable are your cats in their relationship?

Could your cat(s) get on well with a new furry sibling?

Being so similar to their aloof, independent relatives, domestic cats are not necessarily designed to be the social party animal. These wild relatives live solitary lives, hunting small, bite-size prey, which aren't really big enough to share. Indeed, wildcats will mostly keep to themselves just to avoid having to fight over the same scrawny little rodents. Many of the ways cats communicate are via scent and visual markings; this way they can leave each other messages without actually having to be there in person. These include spraying their urine, rubbing their scent glands on things, scratching objects such as the bark of trees and leaving their poo in obvious places (also known as 'middening'). These messages help other cats to determine who was where and when so that they don't accidentally bump into each other. This is very useful because cats don't seem to have a lot of behaviours geared towards diffusing tense situations involving others, so total avoidance may often be the safest policy. The exception to this is when they're feeling a bit frisky, of course; then they might seek each other out for a brief bit of romance.

In general, domestic cats are probably a little less stand-offish than their relatives. In certain situations, they can actually get along quite well together. For example, feral and free-living domestic cats may hang out in gangs (or colonies), often comprised of mostly related females who have grown up together. They may even form 'cat crèches' and help look after each other's kittens. Many pet cats can also seemingly get along like a house on fire, seeking each other out for cuddles at every opportunity. However, where free-living cats are concerned, studies suggest that these gangs only function well when most of the cats have grown up together/are related and when there's enough food to go around. If an intruder tries to join the gang they may be chased off and if food becomes scarce, gang members may decide to go their separate ways.

These same rules apply when it comes to our pet cats; growing up together, being related and having plentiful resources are just as important. Unfortunately, compared to their free-living counterparts, the conditions we expect our pets to coexist under can potentially put a little more pressure on them. Many cats in multi-cat homes won't necessarily have grown up together and we control all their access to food and other resources. We also provide them with a comparatively tiny territory from which they cannot easily leave (especially if we keep them solely indoors). While some cats will prevail, even in the face of such adversity, others might find having to share their house with furry siblings (who may not even be their real siblings anyway) a pretty miserable existence.

The extent to how well our cats cope in these situations will be influenced by their individual personalities, their compatibility with the other cats in the home and how well we manage their environment. When it comes to cat-to-cat interactions, you may find a mixture of different characters all under the same roof. You might get the 'lovers' who seem to get on with everyone, the 'fighters' who always seem to be having problems, and the 'loners' who generally try to keep to themselves. It can also be quite common for cats to get on very well with, or at least tolerate, certain individuals, but at the same time hate the sight of certain other cats. These cats may form their own little 'in crowd' and only choose to hang out with select few individuals. Luckily, there are handy quizzes in this section to help you determine where your cat sits on the cat-loving/hating spectrum and, when things aren't great, what you can do about it. The quizzes have been designed to help you to firstly assess the general type of relationship your cats have and to then delve a little deeper in order to find out exactly what they think about each other. There are also plenty of tips and advice to help you to increase the harmony in your multi-cat home. You can take the quiz as many times as you need to for each of your cats. If you just have two cats, you'll only need to do the quizzes once. For those wondering whether to get an additional cat, the quiz in the final part will help you determine if both you and your cat(s) are ready, and, if you do want another cat, how to choose the right one.

Friends or foes: what kind of relationship do your cats have?

For this part, choose the two cats you wish to understand more and assign them a combined score for each question. By the end of this section, you will have an average score which will tell you more about their relationship and attitude towards each other.

It's 'snooze o'clock'. Are these cats:
(assign one score per cat pair)

A. Curled up in a furry little love ball together even though there are a million different places where they could be sleeping

B. Sleeping near to each other, but there's no fur-on-fur action

C. Sleeping in the same area, but facing away from each other

D. Sleeping as far away from each other as possible

E. One cat was sleeping peacefully until they were unceremoniously turfed off their spot by the other cat

How often do these cats interact?
(assign one score per cat pair)

A. Every day; there's usually quite a lot of mutual appreciation going on, complete with rubbing, grooming and play rituals

B. Some days they might have a little play and/or partake in a quick grooming session

C. They might glance in each other's direction or give each other a quick sniff, just to check they still smell the same

D. One cat sometimes tries to interact with the other, but it's usually very one-sided

E. They're either fighting, shouting and wailing at each other, having a staring contest, one is chasing the other away or they are both trying to avoid each other

How often do you see both your cats in the same room/area of the house? (assign one score per cat pair)

A. Most of the time; they are pretty much joined at the hip!

B. Regularly, although they also enjoy a bit of alone time too

C. Only if they are both partaking in the same activity, i.e. they are after food, attention or a warm place to rest

D. Almost never (perhaps there's a Clark Kent/Superman thing going on here?)

E. If one cat sees the other cat approaching, they will usually clear off, sharpish

F. Or: Often, but they're usually squabbling

Friendly interactions: have you ever observed your cats performing the following behaviours to one another? (tick all that apply)

☐ Deciding to hang out together or share things (e.g. food, beds, sofas, warm spots), even when there are lots of different options to choose from

☐ Waving their furry white flag of peace: tails raised upright when approaching each other, sometimes with a slight kink in the end

☐ Tail wrapping: the cats stand next to each other and their tails become intertwined like two snakes mating

☐ Touching noses (it's a sort of cat handshake)

☐ Allogrooming (i.e. both cats groom each other): either at the same time or they take it in turns

☐ Allorubbing (i.e. both cats rub against each other): either at the same time or they take it in turns

☐ Playing together: this may include stalking, chasing, pouncing and 'rough and tumble', but they should both be equally into it and neither hissing, growling or looking tense

☐ Sleeping in a furry heap together or gently touching while snoozing

☐ Purring or 'chirruping' sweet nothings into each other's ears

How often do you notice any of these signs? (assign one score per cat pair)

A. Pretty much all the time; it's a total cat love-fest in my house

B. Quite often, when they're both in the mood

C. One cat is often keen to be friendly, but it's usually not reciprocated by the other cat, or they mainly just tolerate it

D. I hardly even see them in the same room together

E. Never; they are both too busy hating each other

If your cats could describe their relationship in three words, what would these be? (assign one score per cat)

A. Fun, comforting, reassuring

B. Entertaining, amicable, suitable

C. Tolerable, satisfactory, mediocre

D. Annoying, inconvenient, problematic

E. Awful, scary, horrible

Interpret your cats' score

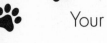

Your cats scored mostly A's and B's
– what does this mean?

Your cats are probably good friends

Your cats are likely to see themselves as being part of the same cat family. They will generally have a friendly, amicable relationship and benefit from each other's company.

While, on the surface, it certainly appears as if your cats are best pals, it's also important to remember that even best friends can sometimes fall out. If your cats are still both quite young, be aware that their personalities can change, especially after they reach sexual or social maturity. It can be quite common for two cats that got on very well as kittens to naturally drift apart and become more aloof or less tolerant of each other as they become adults. Additionally, cats can be extremely good at using very subtle forms of bullying, which may be much harder for us to spot than the more obvious shouting, chasing and fighting. Be sure to keep an eye out for these subtle signs to ensure all continues to go well in your harmonious multi-cat home.

Possible signs of subtle, multi-cat tension include:

🐾 *One cat constantly attempts to play with the other, but it's not reciprocated*

🐾 *One cat frequently grooms the other, but it's not reciprocated*

🐾 *One cat stares at the other (even from across the room)*

🐾 *One cat directly approaches the other (who looks a bit uncomfortable and might hunch up or move away)*

🐾 *One cat lies in front of an important resource, such as the cat flap or food area, lies across the hallway or jumps up onto your lap just as the other cat was about to*

Take the quiz in the next part to see how comfortable your cats both feel around each other.

Your cats scored mostly C's – what does this mean?

Your cats are probably acquaintances

Your cats behave more like colleagues or acquaintances than friends or family. They probably have a mutual agreement of acceptance, but are unlikely to enjoy each other's company a huge amount. When they are in close proximity, this will usually be due to shared interests (e.g. they are both hungry or want your attention) rather than because they actually want to hang out. While there may be no obvious signs of tension between them and they may appear to coexist relatively peacefully, it's unlikely that they actually enjoy living together all that much. Their relationship is probably built on the principles of tolerance and conflict avoidance and this is usually what helps to keep the peace. Be careful not to miss some of the possible, subtle signs of tension between these two.

Possible signs of subtle, multi-cat tension include:

🐾 *One cat constantly attempts to play with the other, but it's not reciprocated*

🐾 *One cat frequently grooms the other, but it's not reciprocated*

🐾 *One cat stares at the other (even from across the room)*

🐾 *One cat directly approaches the other (who looks a bit uncomfortable and might hunch up or move away)*

🐾 *One cat lies in front of an important resource, such as the cat flap or food area, lies across the hallway or jumps up onto your lap just as the other cat was about to*

Take the quiz in the next part to see how comfortable your cats both feel around each other. To learn more about the possible causes of your cats' slightly frosty relationship and some potential multi-cat harmonising strategies you can try out, see the main advice section below.

Your cats scored mostly D's and E's – what does this mean?

Your cats are probably foes

One (or both) of your cats is likely to see the other as an enemy and they are clearly less than thrilled about their current living arrangements. There's really nothing worse than having a housemate you can't stand and it's probably unlikely that they will be able to work things out on their own. The situation between your cats is also likely to compromise their sense of wellbeing (especially for cats that score mostly D's and E's in the next quiz), so it's really important that they get some support from you to try to make things a little easier for them. To learn more about how to assess your cats' wellbeing, make sure you read the advice sections on pages 213–20. To learn more about how comfortable your cats are together, the possible explanations for this, as well some strategies to help make the situation as tolerable for them as possible, take the next quiz.

How comfortable are your cats in their relationship?

In every relationship, things may sometimes be a little unbalanced; for example, one individual may like or dislike the other a little more. Some are generally givers and others takers, and, sadly, sometimes love may go unrequited. Take the quiz in this section to find out exactly how each of your cats feel about the other and how comfortable they are. For these questions, give each cat a separate score.

If you acquired your cats at different times, what were their initial reactions when they first met?

A. Tail raised to attention, lots of sniffing (front and/or back end), some nose touching and perhaps even a few cheeky head rubs or little licks

B. Tail raised, some tentative sniffing, then back to business as usual – is it dinner time?

C. Some crouching and looking tense, avoiding eye contact and pretending to be really interested in other things

D. Lots of crouching and looking tense, initiating a staring contest and possibly some hissing, swiping, quietly creeping or running away

E. A total stand-off: yowling, wailing, growling, hissing, possibly followed by some swiping and chasing

Signs of worry or being uncomfortable: when your cats are in close proximity, do either of them display any of the following? (tick all that apply)

☐ Tail 'swishing' or 'thumping', like an angry snake, usually while holding themselves close to the ground

☐ Blinking, perhaps turning their head to the side, shaking their head or body or licking their nose; brain reset is being attempted

☐ Suddenly deciding they are extremely dirty and launching into a short, frantic grooming session

☐ Skin twitches or ripples as if someone's just walked over their grave

☐ Suddenly going a bit still, doing their best statue impression

☐ A tense or hunched posture, all limbs pressed to their body, their head pulled in as if they no longer have a neck

☐ All four feet firmly planted on the floor as if they're ready to ping off at a moment's notice

☐ Ears flattened down the sides of their head or pressed flat against it like they've suddenly vanished

☐ Performing an exaggerated blink, perhaps followed by a nose-lick 'gulp' or obvious swallow

How often do you notice any of these signs? (assign one score per cat)

A. Never; he or she is usually quite calm and at ease around the other cat

B. Very rarely, and it was probably more to do with other stuff going on in the house

C. Sometimes, especially if both cats are together for any length of time

D. Pretty much all of the time

E. Often, especially when one cat decides to approach the other

Signs of being relaxed and at ease: when your cats are in close proximity, do either of them display any of the following? (tick all that apply)

☐ A relaxed posture, sometimes resting on their side and no obvious tension in the body

☐ Exposing their sacred tummy area (but not accompanied by any paw swiping)

☐ Sleeping deeply and peacefully

☐ A relaxed facial expression, ears pricked and pointed forwards

☐ Eyes gently closed as if appreciating a beautiful piece of music

How often do you notice any of these signs?

A. Pretty much all the time; my cat seems quite relaxed around the other cat

B. Quite often

C. Occasionally, but only because they are completely ignoring the other cat

D. Never

E. Occasionally, when they're not being angsty

Avoidant behaviours: when your cats are in close proximity, do either of them display any of the following? (tick all that apply)

☐ Pretending the other cat doesn't exist

☐ Keeping their distance as if they're allergic to the other cat

☐ Avoiding direct eye contact or facing away from the other cat

☐ Time-sharing; they may have scheduled times for eating, drinking, using their litter trays, sleeping, going outside or getting attention from you, when they know the other cat isn't going to be there

☐ Having their own separate territory; it's as if they drew an imaginary chalk line down the house and they're sticking to their side of it

How often do you notice
any of these signs?

A. Never

B. Occasionally, but only when they need a little 'me time'

C. Regularly

D. Most of the time

E. They always avoid the other cat, unless instigating a standoff, fight or chase

Unfriendly interactions: when your cats are in close proximity, do either of them display any of the following? (tick all that apply)

☐ Staring directly at the other cat, either at close range or from afar; the first one to blink is a loser

☐ Facing the other cat side on with an arched back and puffed up tail, doing their best 'Halloween cat' impression

☐ A Mexican standoff: both cats facing each other, giving death stares, possibly also shouting at each other

☐ One cat standing upright, almost looming over the other cat who may be in a tense, crouched position or lying defensively on their side, paws ready to swipe if necessary

☐ Stalking the other (but more in an 'I want to chase and kill you' than an 'I want to play with you' kind of way)

☐ Chasing the other (who usually obliges by getting the hell out of there, asap)

☐ 'Displacing' the other by forcing them to move aside

☐ 'Blocking' the other cat's access to a resource such as the cat flap, a comfy spot on the sofa, food bowls or even you, by placing themselves in the way

☐ Vigorously grooming the other cat (who's clearly not enjoying it and doesn't reciprocate)

☐ Growling, wailing, yowling or hissing

☐ Physical attacks, including swiping with front legs, pouncing and grabbing, biting and kicking with back legs in a 'raking' fashion. This is likely to be done with more force than in play and may incorporate some of the above sounds

How often do you notice any of these signs?

A. Never; this cat is a real pacifist

B. Very rarely, but it was probably the consequence of a 'play fight' that got a little out of hand

C. Perhaps once or twice, but only when there are lots of stressful things going on at home

D. Often, but this cat is usually the recipient rather than instigator (i.e. the one being stalked, chased, attacked or blocked)

E. Often, and this cat is usually the instigator

Interpret your cat's scores

Your cat scored mostly A's and B's – what does this mean?

Your cat is probably quite comfortable

Your cat probably feels quite relaxed and at ease in the other's company. While this doesn't necessarily mean they're best friends, your cat's intentions are usually quite amicable and friendly and they are most likely laid-back and respectful enough not to cause too much drama.

Your cat scored mostly C's – what does this mean?

Your cat is probably slightly uncomfortable

At times, your cat is probably a little uncomfortable around your other cat and possibly finds their relationship a little strained or inconvenient. It's likely that this cat is quite tolerant, though, and probably just wants to have an easy life, avoiding conflict as much as possible.

Your cat scored mostly D's
– what does this mean?

Your cat is probably very uncomfortable

Your cat may be having a particularly hard time of it. When it comes to cat conflict, they are most often the recipient rather than the instigator. It's possible that their wellbeing may be compromised due to all the cat-angst they seem to be on the receiving end of. This cat will really need your help to feel safer and supported in their multi-cat home. If their situation doesn't improve, then ultimately they may benefit most from being rehomed in a calmer environment where they won't be picked on.

Your cat scored mostly E's
– what does this mean?

Your cat is probably a bit of an antagonist

You're probably already aware of the fact that your cat has a few bullying tendencies; they are likely to be the instigator in most of the conflict that arises between this cat pair. Much of this behaviour may be down to their personality, but also how this cat is feeling both physically and mentally.

Just like in humans, bullies aren't necessarily very happy either, so it's important to consider the wellbeing of this cat too and not to chastise them for their behaviour. After all, they are pretty much behaving just as their wild relatives would in this situation! What this cat's behaviour is suggesting, though, is that they are clearly having trouble sharing their environment with cats and they are likely to have quite a negative impact on the others around them. Ultimately, 'E' cats might be best off living in a single-cat household.

Tips and advice for all cats

Understanding why your cats don't get on

It can be very useful to try to understand the potential reasons why two cats might not like each other that much. These can then help you to decide how best to try to bring more harmony to your multi-cat environment. The following are some of the most common explanations:

- 🐾 **The cat's ancestry:** *Because cats are still so closely related to their solitary, territorial relatives, their brains may often still be programmed to see most cats as foes rather than friends.*

- 🐾 **The cat's previous experiences:** *If a cat has been well-socialised with other cats as kittens and then* *continues to have nice experiences with cats as they grow up, they may be much more likely to accept living with other cats as an adult. On the other hand, if your cat(s) went straight from the nest as a kitten to living in a single-cat household, they might find suddenly having to live with another cat very difficult to accept as an adult. Additionally, if your cats have only ever had bad experiences with other cats in the past, before being introduced to each other, they may be less likely to readily accept one another.*

🐾 ***Their personality:*** *Just like us, the personalities of some cats can clash, meaning they just don't get on. It may be that if you have two very active, bold and confident cats, they are more likely to clash than if you have two very shy, quiet or generally laid-back cats. If two cats have very similar likes and dislikes, this might also cause more tension and competition between them; they might want to use the same things at the same times and not necessarily want to share.*

🐾 ***Their family tree:*** *A cat's personality is partially shaped by that of their parents; if your cat has parents that were generally hostile and unfriendly towards other cats, this may increase the chances of your cat showing similar tendencies.*

🐾 ***Age differences:*** *Kittens will usually be more tolerant of other cats and often become less tolerant as they age (perhaps just like humans?!). Studies suggest that, in general, older cats might find sharing their living quarters with other cats more challenging. Kittens might also be better accepted by adult cats, although youngsters tend to be more active and brazen, keen to tear around the house and engage in some rough and tumble. This might be quite annoying for your grandpa and grandma cats who are just looking for a quiet life, undisturbed.*

🐾 ***Their mental health:*** *If cats live in a stressful environment where they feel unsafe, agitated or uncertain a lot of the time, this can potentially make sharing their lives with other furry creatures quite challenging. When times are hard, cats will very rarely look to one another for support; most of the time they will, in fact, do the exact opposite, avoiding social interactions in favour of focusing on keeping themselves safe.*

🐾 ***Their physical health:*** *If one of your cats is physically unwell or in pain, they may want to avoid interactions with other cats because they just aren't in the mood or because this might cause them further pain.*

🐾 ***Their hormones:*** *If any of your cats aren't neutered, they are likely to have higher levels of both sex and stress-related hormones coursing through their little furry bodies. This may cause them to experience more stress and tension in multi-cat environments, leading to increased conflict and territorial disputes between cats.*

🐾 ***Their environment:*** *Cats are more likely to experience conflict and competition with other cats when they are forced to be in close proximity or have to share all of their resources. Most cats will particularly prefer to perform activities such as eating, drinking and toileting alone and undisturbed, so the last thing they want is a small furry audience while they're going about their business. If your cats have a genuine dislike for each other, in reality, they may prefer to perform ALL of their daily activities away from one another!*

🐾 ***Current cat social dynamics:*** *Each cat will add something different to the dynamics within your multi-cat home. However, some 'big personality' cats might influence things more than the quiet, timid ones. Where a big, laid-back, confident softie might be the glue that keeps your small cat gang together, a bold, brazen, bully cat might be the cause of a lot of* *cat drama, even among cats that might otherwise get along. It's often the case that when one cat is no longer around, the dynamics among the remaining cats may change a great deal, usually for the better if the absent cat was the one causing trouble.*

How to help increase the harmony in your multi-cat home

First and foremost, <u>under no circumstances</u> should you try to discipline any cats for their angsty behaviour – no cats are mean just for the sake of it and it's much better to take the side of compassion than punishment. Additionally, any shouting or physically disturbing the cats is only likely to increase their anxiety levels rather than reduce them, having the opposite effect from the one you want

If your cats do get into fights, the best thing to do is to strategically slide something in between them to block their view of each other (e.g. a big piece of cardboard), then physically separate them. If they are already mid-tussle, try placing a towel over one or both of them, which should help to disrupt things long enough for one cat to make a quick getaway (you might also be able to scoop one of the cats up in the towel)

The best way to determine your best 'cat harmonising strategies' is to firstly take stock of the situation by starting to build up a picture of the dynamics within your multi-cat group (this is especially useful if you have more than two cats):

🐾 *Use your answers from the first part of the quiz to determine the quality of the relationships between each of your cats; does one cat mostly have 'friends' or 'acquaintances' where another mainly has 'foes'?*

🐾 *Use your answers from the second part to determine how comfortable your cats generally seem around each other. If there's trouble, is one cat usually the antagoniser and one the victim? Is there a particular cat that's very uncomfortable around most of the others?*

🐾 *It's a great idea to draw a 'social network' diagram (like the one opposite). This will help you to get a better overview of what's going on with your furry cat bunch. You may also be able to identify if you have any 'lovers', 'fighters', 'loners' or cats that have formed their own little in crowd.*

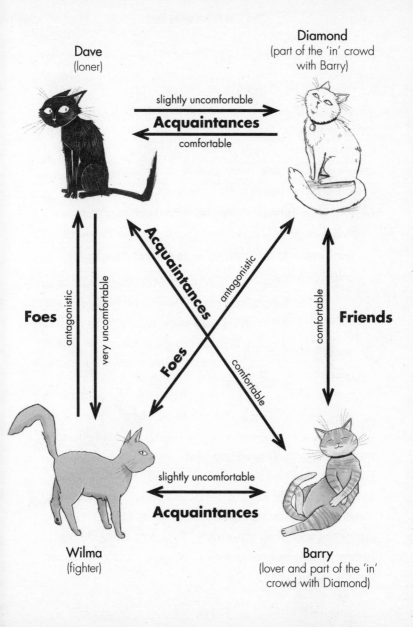

Barry

In this scenario, Barry is a 'lover'. He's friends with Diamond and on 'acquaintance' terms with both Dave and Wilma. He has comfortable relationships with the other cats, except Wilma (who can be a tricky customer). He spends most of his time with Diamond, forming a two-cat 'in crowd'.

Diamond

Diamond is friends with Barry and is an 'acquaintance' of Dave's; he has comfortable relationships with both cats. He actively dislikes Wilma, however, whom he considers his 'foe' and they occasionally antagonise each other.

Dave

Dave is a 'loner'. He is an 'acquaintance' of both Diamond and Barry. He is generally most comfortable around Barry, but less so with Diamond and usually tries to stay out of the way of all other cats. He is also being bullied by Wilma, whom he considers his 'foe', and feels very uncomfortable around her.

Wilma

Wilma is a 'fighter' as she is antag-
onistic towards both Dave and
Diamond who are her 'foes'. She and
Barry are 'acquaintances' but she feels
slightly uncomfortable around him and
generally tries to avoid him.

If you have a mix of 'fighters', 'loners', and 'in-crowd cats',
and the space in your house allows, it's likely that they will
have carved out several separate territories for themselves,
mainly to try to avoid each other. Try to work out where each
cat spends most of their time and who may or may not share
the same territory. Drawing a simple house map like the one
below is useful.

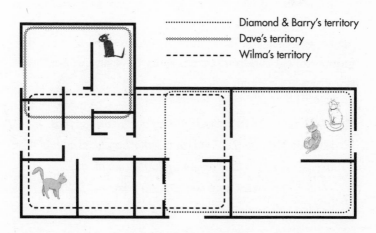

```
············· Diamond & Barry's territory
∞∞∞∞∞∞∞∞∞ Dave's territory
- - - - - - - Wilma's territory
```

🐾 *Your cats should ideally be neutered. Also ensure they are also in good physical health; a trip to the vets might be necessary to rule out any underlying medical problems if you have any concerns.*

Use the quiz on pages 181–222 to help assess the wellbeing of each cat in your multi-cat home, exploring the following questions:

🐾 *Are there certain cats that appear to be particularly struggling with multi-cat-living (for example, the 'loners' and 'fighters', like Dave and Wilma)?*

🐾 *Are all the basic needs for each cat being properly met?*

🐾 *If not, is there anything you can do to better meet these needs?*

Assess whether you have enough resources to support the number of cat children you currently have and where these resources are located:

🐾 *Make sure you have multiples of all the things that your cats' value (i.e. food and water bowls; sleeping areas; places to hide or get up high; warm, quiet spots; litter trays, toys, scratching posts etc.). The golden rule is one of each per cat, plus a few extras.*

🐾 *Make sure each cat can access all of their valued resources without having to share them or cross paths with the other cats to get to them (especially their 'acquaintances' and 'foes'). If your cats have separate territories, make sure each territory contains sufficient resources for the number of cats within it.*

🐾 *Even within the same territory, avoid clumping all of the resources together. Place food, water bowls and litter trays in separate areas – even cats have qualms about pooing near to their dinner table.*

🐾 *Your cats might use their smell and claws to 'reinforce' their territory, so avoid cleaning their sleeping areas and objects they rub against too often. Additionally, provide materials for them to scratch, placing them in prominent locations, such as at the boundaries of their territory.*

🐾 *Cats may feel most vulnerable when they are a little distracted (e.g. eating, drinking or toileting, or when they are sleeping). Position these associated resources in a way that your cat can feel safe when using them and has a clear view of any potential threats coming their way. For example, place food bowls on a raised surface or cat tree, avoid using litter trays with covers over them and place blankets on shelves or on the top of cupboards for your cats to use.*

🐾 *Ensure that one cat cannot block another cat's access to these resources (e.g. avoid placing them at the end of a narrow corridor with no option for a quick escape).*

🐾 *Ensure that one cat cannot block another cat's access to parts of the house or to the outdoors. For example, provide your cats with multiple entry and exit points to the different areas of the house or install multiple cat flaps to the outdoors in separate locations.*

🐾 *You could try to provide the more vulnerable cats with access to safe areas within the home where they can go without any risk of being disturbed or bullied. For example, keep the door to one room in your house permanently closed and install a microchip cat flap that is only programmed to open for selected cats.*

🐾 *If your cats enjoy lots of play and attention, ensure you schedule each of them in separately for regular, quality 'you time'.*

🐾 *Try to make your cats' indoor and outdoor environment as enriching and stimulating as possible, keeping them busy and out of mischief. See pages 167–170 for advice on how to do this.*

If the age gap between some of your cats is an issue (e.g. you have a young, boisterous cat that keeps pestering your older, slightly arthritic cat), here are a few suggestions on how to help:

🐾 *Make sure your older cat is being treated for any underlying painful conditions*

🐾 *Make sure you give the young scamp plenty to do in order to occupy their active little mind and tire them out (see advice on pages 167–70 for more advice)*

🐾 *Create areas of the house exclusively for your older cat (e.g. a room or area with access via a microchip cat flap)*

Sometimes tension in multi-cat homes can be caused just as much by the cats outside your home as those inside. Ensure there aren't intruder cats sneaking into your house through an open door or window. If you have a cat flap, make sure it's microchip-operated so your cats have exclusive access. If there are lots of cats in the neighbourhood, try to discourage them from hanging around in your garden. For example, avoid feeding or giving them attention, try 'shooing' them away, or even placing some of your cat's poo around the perimeter of your garden to help him or her better mark the edges of their territory. Make sure there are a lot of places your cats can hide and get up high so that they feel safer when outdoors. You might even want to consider 'cat proofing' your garden by placing special fencing along its perimeter, to stop unwanted cats getting in.

When you have implemented all your new 'cat harmonising strategies', make sure you keep an eye on each cat and continue to track their progress. You can repeat the above quizzes as well as the one on pages 181–222 and compare their scores over time – are things generally changing in a positive direction or are certain cats still struggling? You may find that additional support from a suitably qualified cat behaviour counsellor is useful.

Finally, be prepared to accept that, if your cats fundamentally dislike each other or their personalities clash, there may be very little you can actually do to change their minds about each other. While better management of their environment can certainly help to relieve a lot of the tension, it can only go so far. Sometimes the best way to improve the harmony and wellbeing for all cats concerned is to rehome the ones that continue to struggle or those that cause the majority of problems. While this can be an extremely difficult thing to do, it might just be the kindest thing.

Could your cat(s) get on with a furry sibling? (And are you ready for another cat?)

Why do you want to get another cat?

A. You like the idea of having another cat to interact with; your house and garden are big enough to support an additional cat and you think your current cat(s) would accept another really well

B. Your current cat(s) has always got on well living with other cats

C. You think your current cat(s) is lonely since your last one passed away

D. You want to add a bit of diversity into the mix; a different breed or colour of cat would fit well into your home

E. Your cat is behaving aggressively and you think a furry playmate would help them to calm down a bit

What would your new cat's territory look like?

A. A large house with lots of different rooms and a big garden

B. A medium-sized house with various rooms and an average-sized garden

C. A small house: several rooms and a small garden

D. A flat: a few rooms and a small garden

E. A flat: a few rooms and no garden

Who currently lives in your household?

A. 1 cat and 1–2 humans

B. 2 cats and 1–2 humans

C. 1–2 cats and 3 or more humans

D. 3–4 cats and 1–3 humans

E. 5 or more cats and 1 or more humans

You're deciding what kind of cat
to add to your household. Do you:

A. Carefully consider the personality of your current
   cat(s), how well they all get on and the type of
   cat (i.e. age, personality) they may most likely
   accept well

B. Decide on a calm, friendly looking, laid-back cat

C. Decide on a young, boisterous kitten to inject some
   life into your cat group

D. Pick the cutest-looking cat you can find

E. Go for the feistiest-looking cat with the most 'cattitude'

How busy is your household?

A. Generally quiet, peaceful and routine-like

B. Mostly calm and peaceful

C. There are some busy, hectic times, followed by quiet periods

D. It's usually quite lively; there's always something going on or people visiting

E. It's usually very chaotic and unpredictable

If you already have a multi-cat household, how well do these cats get on? (use their scores from parts 1 and 2 above to help you answer this question)

A. All of the cats are 'friends' and are comfortable around each other

B. Most of the cats are 'friends' and seem comfortable around each other

C. Most of the cats are 'acquaintances' or seem slightly uncomfortable around each other

D. Some of the cats are 'foes', 'antagonists' or seem very uncomfortable around each other

E. Most of the cats are 'foes', 'antagonists' or are very uncomfortable around each other

What is the personality of your current cat(s) like?

A. Super friendly, laid-back and easygoing

B. Cool, calm and collected

C. Amenable, tolerant, but can be a little jumpy at times

D. Anxious, on edge and very sensitive

E. Tense, highly strung and easily annoyed

If you currently have a single-cat
household, has your cat lived
with other cats previously?

A. They have usually always lived with at least one other
    furry sibling since a kitten and they got on like a
    house on fire

B. Yes, and they mostly got on quite well

C. No, they've been an only cat since they were a kitten
    Or: My cat was a stray so I know very little about
    their past

D. No, but they see other cats regularly in the garden
    and they usually end up fighting or shouting at
    each other

E. Yes, and they hated every single second of it

Is/are your current cat(s) neutered?

A. Yes, all of them and they have been since kittens

B. Yes, quite recently

C. You don't know

D. Only some of them

E. No, none of them

How would you describe the general wellbeing of your current cat(s)? (see the quiz on pages 181–222 if you need help answering this question)

A. They seem very happy, contented and relaxed

B. In general, they seem pretty comfortable

C. Sometimes they seem fine; other times maybe a bit uncomfortable

D. They mainly seem a bit anxious, on edge or miserable

E. They always seem very stressed and unhappy

What's the physical health of your current cat(s) like?

A. Active, healthy and pain-free

B. Mostly active, healthy and pain-free

C. A few minor health issues but they're responding well to treatment

D. A few serious health issues but they're responding well to treatment

E. They have an ongoing health issue and are struggling quite a lot

How would you plan to introduce your new cat to your existing cat(s)?

A. Slowly, carefully and in stages, making sure all the cats are comfortable. You're prepared for it to take months if necessary

B. Gradually, over the course of a few weeks

C. You'll just do what feels right when the time comes

D. Open the carrier door then let them do their own thing

E. Shut them in the kitchen together – the sooner they can deal with each other the better!

How would you ensure your cats all
have enough opportunities to stay out
of each other's fur if they want to?

A. There will be plenty of separate places for each of
   them to eat, drink, toilet, sleep, rest, play and spy on
   their humans, undisturbed

B. If they decide they want their own territories, you'll
   make sure you distribute their resources accordingly

C. You'll make sure you feed them in different locations

D. They'll have to work that out for themselves

E. Your home doesn't allow for a lot of separate spaces
   – they will just have to learn how to share

Interpret your score

You scored mostly A's and B's
– what does this mean?

All signs suggest that you and your cat(s) are well positioned to welcome another furry family member. You potentially have a great, cat-friendly set up in your home and your current cat(s) is likely to be well-provided-for and comfortable, and would potentially adjust well to a new arrival. However, not much in life is guaranteed, so it's still really important that you follow the advice and recommendations below, ensuring you choose the right cat and give them the very best possible chance of a smooth and happy integration into your home. Cats can be very specific in their likes and dislikes, so even if your existing cats currently get on very well together, there's no guarantee they will feel the same way about a new arrival.

You scored mostly C's
– what does this mean?

Circumstances may be less than optimal where the addition of more cat children to your family is concerned. Your environment may not be the best to support harmonious multi-cat living and your existing cat(s) may potentially find this quite challenging. It's therefore worth thinking a little more carefully about if this is the right time to be acquiring more cats and, if you did, whether this would compromise the wellbeing of your current ones. However, if your heart is still truly set on getting another cat, it's particularly important that you take heed of the tips and advice overleaf.

You scored mostly D's and E's – what does this mean?

The signs suggest that acquiring another cat might not be the best idea. Where, as cat owners, we may often think the more cats the merrier, we mustn't forget that, just like their relatives, when it comes to being around other cats, some individuals prefer to be lone rangers. Multi-cat living can be difficult at the best of times, but it's made considerably worse if cats have only a small territory, their resources are limited or not well-distributed, there are lots of busy humans around or they have to share with lots of other cats (especially those that are anxious, stressed, or unwell). While some cats may be able to cope with a lot of what we throw at them, it doesn't necessarily mean they are happy about it. Now is probably the time for you to focus on making sure your existing cat(s) is as happy as possible rather than thinking about adding extra ones into the mix.

Tips and advice for all answers

Choosing the right cat

If you think your cat is ready to accept another into the fold, the next step is to choose the right kind of sibling for them. In an ideal world, it's better to acquire all the cats in your multi-cat household at the same time, as kittens. However, if you already have one or more cats and want to add another, the next best options are to:

🐾 *Choose a young, calm kitten who appears to get on well with its litter mates and (if you can find out) has parents who also got on well with other cats*

🐾 *Or: choose an older cat that has lived with other cats before and always got on very well with them*

🐾 *Choose a cat whose personality and activity levels are likely to complement those of your existing cat(s):*

- *If you have a lot of old, sedentary grandpa and grandma cats, avoid a very boisterous young cat (unless you are prepared to be their new, dedicated playmate!)*

- *If you already have a very lively, playful cat, a young, active, confident kitten may be a good match*

- *If you have an anxious, skittish cat, a calm, confident, laid-back cat may be the best match*
- *Avoid choosing a cat based on its breed alone as this is no guarantee of its behaviour or personality*

Preparing your home

Make sure you've provided enough resources for all of your cats and these are well-distributed around the house. Ensure access to them cannot be easily blocked by any of your cats. Provide plenty of quiet, 'safe' places for your cats to go (i.e. places they can hide or get up high) if they feel under threat.

Before your new cat arrives, create a small, individual territory for them by placing everything they need (food, water, litter trays, beds, hiding places, toys and scratching posts) in a quiet room in your home. It's best to buy new items for your new cat rather than taking away belongings from your existing cats.

Introductions

This should be done gradually and in stages, allowing the cats to get to know each other slowly, in their own time. During introductions, it's totally fine if your new and existing cats don't want to play together or even interact at all, so never force them to be in close proximity to, or touch, each other. If at any stage things don't go well between them, go back a stage or two in the introduction process and progress at a slower pace.

❧ *When your new cat arrives, settle them into their little territory, close the door and leave them to chill for a couple of hours.*

❧ *After a few days, or when you think they're suitably comfortable in their new digs, place an item belonging to your existing cats, such as a blanket they sleep on, in your new cat's room, with some tasty treats next to it. Make sure the blanket is used, so it has your existing cat's smell on it. Do the same with your existing cat(s), leaving them a blanket with your new cat's smell on for them to investigate, with the accompanying treats, of course.*

❧ *Swap these blankets back and forth between cats for at least a couple of days.*

❧ *When you feel your new cat is happy and relaxed in their room and that both new and existing cats have accepted the other's smell (i.e. they no longer pay any attention to the blankets when you swap them over), you can start letting your new cat explore the rest of their home for short periods of time. Leave the door to your new cat's room open so that they can always retreat if they get a bit overwhelmed. Make sure your existing cats aren't around (i.e. wait until they are exploring outside and fix the cat flap shut or keep them in the bedroom with you overnight if they won't mind this restriction too much). If this all goes well, repeat this a few times over a couple of days.*

🐾 *Next, start to let the cats have just a peek at each other (look but don't touch). Either open the door to the new cat's room a tiny crack and fix it in place or open the door fully, but secure a tall piece of mesh or a see-through plastic barrier in the doorway so that neither cat can physically get to the other.*

🐾 *Use treats to create positive associations when the cats are in each other's presence, but don't encourage them to eat directly next to each other – as cats usually prefer to eat alone.*

🐾 *Pay attention to their behaviour and body language. If you notice any signs that either cat is uncomfortable (see the quiz sections above), lure one away and end their introduction session.*

🐾 *If all does go well, repeat the sessions often over a couple of days.*

🐾 *If both cats appear relaxed when in close proximity (see the quiz sections above), open the door to the new cat's room and allow them to have supervised meet and greets. Use treats (a separate pile for each cat) and play (a separate toy for each) to encourage them to feel comfortable and happy around each other.*

🐾 *If these sessions go well, progress to unsupervised cat meetings, but check in on them every so often to make sure things are still going all right. If all continues to go to plan, repeat these sessions often, over a couple of days.*

🐾 *If all cats seem happy and there have been no incidents between either of them, keep the new cat's room permanently open and let all cats come and go as they please. Make sure your new cat still has access to this room and that all their belongings stay inside so that they still have a nice, safe space to retreat to if they need it.*

🐾 *Keep an eye on how all the cats are doing and follow the advice sections in the first part for long-term 'cat harmonising strategies'.*

🐾 *Careful selection of the right cat plus a gradual introduction will give your cats the best possible chances of getting on well. However, if, once fully introduced, the new or existing cat is making the other miserable, you've already implemented all the 'cat harmonising strategies' and/or sought advice from a qualified cat behaviour counsellor, it may be that your new cat just isn't compatible with the others and needs rehoming.*

Science corner

Do cats form hierarchies? Are some cats more 'dominant' than others?

Solitary wildcats don't live in complex cat communities, with chiefs and deputies, so it stands to reason that the domestic cat didn't inherit this ability from their relatives. Studies of free-living domestic cats in the wild find no evidence of clear 'dominance hierarchies'. While older, unneutered males may try to stop juvenile males from breeding, females will usually cooperate and may even help to rear others' young. It seems that, when it comes to politics, cats are more likely to form socialist coalitions than dictatorships. While some cats may certainly seem to bully others, this doesn't necessarily mean they are completely 'dominant' over them, rather that they may just be more intolerant of multi-cat living or that they need to feel more in control of the resources in their home and so try to stop others from using them.

Do cats grieve for each other?

Scientifically, we still don't really know enough about cats' brains and their emotions to be able to answer this question. However, anecdotally, many people describe their cat's behaviour changing quite drastically when one cat passes away or leaves the home. While some cats that were super bonded may certainly miss the social interaction and comfort that the other provided, they probably don't grieve in the same way that humans do. There are also a few other plausible explanations behind the behaviour changes we may witness in our cats:

🐾 *The remaining cat(s) might be picking up on changes in our moods and general behaviour, which could cause them stress. In addition, they might suddenly receive a lot more attention from us than usual. If they aren't much of a love bug (see quizzes on pages 6–35 and 36–59), they could find this rather unpleasant or overwhelming.*

🐾 *The dynamics within your multi-cat household may have shifted. If your cats were previously 'time-sharing' certain areas of the house, they may have adjusted their schedules slightly, now there's one less cat around.*

🐾 *The departed cat may have been a bit of a bully or 'resource blocker' and suddenly your remaining cats feel better able to use their environment as they please. This can also mean that, now, you too appear much more available to them so they might start asking for a lot more cuddles than usual!*

SECTION 3:
THE HUNTER CAT

How predatory or playful is your cat?

As sweet and innocent-looking as our furry companions are, when it comes to unleashing their predatory side, there's little room for mercy. As a species, the domestic cat is often still an extremely effective predator of all small creatures, be they scaled, feathered or covered in fur. Interestingly, the desire and ability for cats to hunt is thought to be relatively hard-wired in their brains. However, some cats might have a particular advantage if they had the chance to perfect their hunting skills as kittens. In the wild, food can be a scarce commodity so you can't always wait until you're hungry to check out the menu. If cats don't seize every chance they get, they're likely to regret it later, especially given that probably only half of all their hunting attempts are actually successful. This goes a long way towards explaining why even cats that are fed the best gourmet food might still get the urge to seek out scrawny little mice to hunt after.

A lot of what cats do when they play is largely based on their arsenal of hunting skills. Whether this be with us, their toys, our new sofa or even other pets, you're likely to see a lot of the same types of predatory moves. What can be tricky for us is to balance the ingrained desires of our cats against our own needs to keep our hands and feet intact, have nice-looking furniture and avoid the total decimation of our local wildlife. Additionally, some cats might seem as if they are really up for a play session, but tend to get bored very quickly. Luckily, here's a handy quiz you can take to help you determine how predatory/playful your cat likely is as well as plenty of tips and advice to help you to manage them, wherever they fall on the spectrum, be it extreme predator or unenthusiastic playmate.

You've had a long day at work and could do with a fun, distracting play session with your cat. Is your cat:

A. In position and standing to attention – paws are engaged and ready!

B. Only a brief shake of the toy basket away

C. Ready and willing as long as there are guaranteed to be treats involved

D. Likely sleeping or pretending to ignore you

E. Running away as soon as they hear the toy basket come out – there's nothing worse than play time with you

It's been a while since you last had a good play session with your cat. Do you notice your cat doing any of the following? (tick all that apply)

- [ ] Looking restless, pacing and meowing

- [ ] Pouncing on you while you're sleeping

- [ ] Attacking your hands and feet

- [ ] Ambushing you from behind a curtain as you walk past

- [ ] Tormenting the other pets in the house with endless stalking, chasing, pouncing or trying to engage them in some rough and tumble

- [ ] Seemingly becoming possessed by the cat-devil, tearing around the house, literally bouncing off the walls, getting spooked by imaginary creatures

- [ ] Taking matters into their own hands and trying to hunt invisible objects

How often do any of these behaviours happen?

A. Without fail – play time is even more important than nap time for your cat

B. Often, although the situation can usually be remedied by chucking a toy mouse in their direction

C. Only occasionally; your cat generally seems pretty good at entertaining themselves

D. Perhaps once; your cat is usually too preoccupied with eating and sleeping to bother with any of that play business

E. Never; your cat clearly has other priorities

How often do you see evidence of your cat's hunting endeavours (for example, he or she brings you furry little 'presents' or you find a small pile of feathers somewhere)?

A. In the spring and summer months it's pretty much a daily occurrence

B. It happens quite often – what did you do to deserve all these gifts?!

C. It may happen occasionally, but probably only when your cat gets lucky

D. It might have happened once, although you're pretty sure your cat probably found something that was already dead and then just pretended they caught it themselves

E. Never; you're wondering if your cat might be a secret vegetarian
Or: You have an indoor cat and would be *very* surprised by a furry gift!

Your cat is sitting at the window and there's a bird perched very close on the other side of the glass, preening its feathers. Does your cat:

A. Start making that weird, open-mouthed 'chittering' noise as if they're a cat robot that's malfunctioning

B. Assume the crouched, stalking position, focusing intently on their subject

C. Look quite interested, but relatively relaxed, enjoying the free entertainment

D. Glance in the bird's direction, probably just to humour it

E. Do nothing – oh, is there a bird outside? I hadn't noticed …

How long does the average play session with your cat last?

A. As long as you can stand it – your cat could probably play for eternity if you let him/her

B. They can usually keep going for a good 20 minutes or so

C. You're likely to be able to keep them entertained for about 5–10 minutes, as long as you keep moving the toy in the right way and mix it up a bit with a few different toys

D. You might get a few half-hearted paw-bats out of them if you're lucky

E. They would really rather you just gave them food

How enthusiastically does your cat play (with mouse-like prey)?

Use your cat's favourite toy, or preferably a fishing rod/wand with a mouse-sized object on the end, covered in either feathers or soft furry material. The toy should ideally be something your cat hasn't encountered before or a toy you know they really like, but don't get to play with often.

Politely get your cat's attention. Drag the toy slowly and then quickly along the ground in a straight line, using short bursts of sporadic movement with a brief pause in between. Allow your cat to 'catch' the end of the toy occasionally, but keep moving it as if there's a real mouse on the end, trying to escape. Try to keep the 'mouse' on or close to the ground. Observe your cat for 60 seconds while you move the toy. Ideally you should perform this test on several occasions at different times of the day to get a more accurate picture of your cat's behaviour.

Did your cat (tick all of the following you observe):

☐ Intently focus on the toy, whiskers and ears alert and forwards, like an antenna locking on to a new signal

☐ Begin stalking the toy, approaching quickly while in a couched position – body held close to the ground

☐ Start to lift their back legs up and down as if the ground is suddenly a bit too hot (it might also look as if they are trying to wiggle their bum). In addition, you might see their tail get a bit twitchy

☐ Briefly sprint towards the 'prey', finishing with a pounce or spring as they try to catch it

☐ Use one or both of their front paws to strike at the 'prey' or briefly pin it to the ground

☐ Deliver a killing bite by sinking their canines into the 'prey' (possibly at the nape of its neck – if it has one!)

☐ 'Rake' furiously at the toy with their back legs, the toy either clasped in their mouth or between their front paws

☐ Clasp the toy in their mouth and attempt to carry it off

☐ Toss the toy about and/or bat at it with their paws

◻ Start to 'pluck' the fur or feathers (whether real or imaginary) from the toy, using their teeth

Did they:

A. Execute most of these behaviours with military precision

B. Perform at least several of these behaviours, perhaps some a little clumsily

C. Perform one or two of these behaviours, although their enthusiasm was a little lacking at times

D. Give the toy a half-hearted bat with their paw once – does that count?!

E. Observe you mockingly from a distance; this was the extent of their participation

How enthusiastically does your cat play (with flying prey)?

Use the same wand toy as in the previous tests or one that has a bird- or insect-looking object on the end. Politely get your cat's attention. Using your best puppetry skills, try to move the toy about like a small bird or winged insect, flying from one location to another. For example, you can let it 'land' on the ground and/or nearby furniture every so often. Alter the height of your flying creature so that sometimes it's at your cat's height and other times your cat will have to jump up to catch it. Allow your cat to 'catch' the toy occasionally, but keep moving it as if there's a real creature on the end, trying to escape. Observe your cat for 60 seconds while you move the toy around.* Ideally, you should perform this test on several occasions at different times of the day to get a more accurate picture of your cat's behaviour.

* If your cat isn't convinced by this activity, avoid continuously dangling the toy in their face to get a reaction. This is likely to cause maximum annoyance to your cat and may give false results (i.e. your cat might swat at the toy simply to get it out of their face).

Did your cat:

A. Repeatedly spring off the ground like a tiny rocket, performing a series of acrobatic leaps, twists and summersaults

B. Jump up and attempt to catch the toy a few times, especially when it flew nearby or 'landed'

C. Refrain from jumping up but gave the toy a few bats with their paw when it was in reach

D. Assume a crouched position, orientating their head or body towards the toy to keep an eye on it

E. Observe you mockingly from a distance, the extent of their participation

How easily is your cat distracted with toys?

Use some of your cat's favourite treats and the same toy as in the previous test. Place a small pile of treats near to them. Allow your cat to approach and let them start eating the treats. Move about a metre away and begin to move the fishing rod/wand toy in the same way as described in either of the previous tests. Keep moving the wand for 30 seconds.

Did your cat:

A. Leap into action as soon as the toy started to twitch, the treats sent flying

B. Quickly turn to face the toy, going into stalk mode, getting ready to make their move

C. Leisurely head over to investigate, but quickly lose interest and head back to the food

D. Briefly look up in the direction of the toy, but then continue to polish off the treats

E. Keep their head down, focusing on the task at hand
Or: My cat isn't interested in eating when I'm around

Interpret your cat's score

Your cat scored mostly A's and B's – what does this mean?

Your cat is likely to be an incredibly playful little fellow. One wiggle of a piece of string is probably enough to send them into full-on attack mode. You may find that he or she is often quite alert and aware of their surroundings, responding inquisitively to sudden movements and sounds. In general, your cat may have a strong drive to explore, craving lots of brain stimulation and physical activity. While some cats might be sufficiently satisfied to focus their energies predominantly on toys and other non-living objects, many highly playful/predatory cats will also be attracted to the real deal.

Read on to learn some of the best ways to keep your cat sufficiently entertained and also how to potentially dissuade them from hunting quite so much.

How can you keep your cat sufficiently entertained?

The great indoors

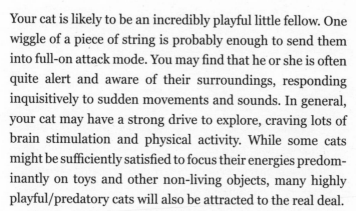

🐾 *Cats with a thirst for exploration and adventure will also benefit from a stimulating indoor environment.*

This will be particularly crucial where the cat is unable to have access to an exciting, outdoor space.

🐾 *Again, most cats enjoy having the opportunity to hang out and explore at different heights, so shelves and large cat-trees dotted about the place are ideal, in addition to some concealed places where they can hide.*

🐾 *When it comes to feeding time, this can also be made more exciting by placing the cat's usual food into puzzle feeders: different feeders can be used for both wet and dry food. Your cat may enjoy both the stationary and moveable ones or have a preference for a specific kind, so you may need to experiment a bit to find out what they like. You can easily buy a range of different puzzle feeders, but, if you're feeling creative, you could try making your own!*

🐾 *Using puzzle feeders will give your cat both mental and physical exercise; they're especially good for cats prone to boredom, those that tend to eat their food too quickly and cats that simply need to move about more. The best strategy is to have a few different kinds on rotation to keep things exciting for your cat.*

🐾 *While your cat may always be up for a chance to unleash their playful/predatory side, you can make sure play time stays as exciting as possible by mixing up the toys you use to keep things as novel and fun as possible. Toys loaded with cat nip or valerian may be particularly stimulating as they add an additional sensory element.*

🐾 *Your cat will probably get very excited when in play mode. When playing with your cat, using a wand and fishing rod-type toy will help your cat to avoid mistaking your hands or feet for their prey in the heat of the moment. Indeed, never encourage your cat to 'play' with your hands or feet as this is likely to be a hard habit for them to break once established and can become quite painful and/or annoying for you!*

The great outdoors

🐾 *In general, cats benefit greatly from having a stimulating outdoor environment to explore. They will really appreciate and enjoy all the sights, sounds and smells that the great outdoors has to offer; especially if their garden also provides them with a sense of safety (for example bushes to hide in and good, high-up vantage points).*

🐾 *Providing a range of insect-attracting plants, in addition to cat-attracting ones (such cat grass, honeysuckle, cat mint, valerian and cat nip), will all be excellent for stimulating your cat's senses.*

🐾 *Placing a bit of furniture in the garden at different levels will add extra exciting dimensions to the garden as well as allow your cat to safely spy on any potential intruders. Wooden shelves attached to a wall or fence, chairs and tables, or even purpose-built cat houses are all excellent choices.*

🐾 *If you're worried about the safety of your cat when they're outside, there are plenty of ways to help keep them safe and close by. The more exciting their garden is, the less likely they are to roam further afield. You could try teaching your cat a recall so that you can easily get them to come back to you. Fitting your cat with a specially designed GPS collar will also help you to keep track of their movements.*

🐾 *Additionally, there are various ways that gardens can be 'cat proofed' (for example by placing special fencing along its perimeter, to stop cats getting in or out), ensuring your cat stays where you can see them.*

How can I discourage their predatory ways when outside?

Because of their hard-wiring, it's probably impossible to completely diminish your cat's desire to hunt. However, the above strategies may all help to give them enough of an outlet to keep these urges at bay when outdoors. The following advice may also help:

🐾 ***Cats thrive on variety:*** *While we may tend to feed our cats the same food each meal, most cats are inherently drawn towards variety. The more monotonous their daily meals, the more likely they may be to go out looking for more interesting things to munch on. Spicing things up in the kitchen by providing them with a range of flavours, shapes and textures (e.g. both wet and dry food and alternating between different types of each) at meal times can make things a lot more fun for your cat. Some cats are obviously fussier that others so it might take a bit of trial and error to find a few different foods that your cat finds equally acceptable! Keep any eye on their tummies, though, as some cats can be a little sensitive to lots of sudden changes in their diet.*

🐾 ***Cats prefer good food:*** *Cats that are fed good-quality cat foods, complete with all the nutrients they require, may feel less of a need to go out and 'top up' their diets with creatures from the garden.*

🐾 ***Cats hunt most at dusk and dawn:*** *Studies show that, in the UK at least, small mammals (e.g. mice) are the most popular dish on the menu, followed by birds; although some cats will undoubtedly have exotic tastes and prefer other types of prey. Given the chance, you might find that your cat is more likely to hunt when their preferred prey is most active. For the majority of cats this will be in the early hours of the morning and early evening. Ensuring your cat has plenty to do (i.e. toys to play with and puzzle feeders to get food from), especially at these times, may help to subdue their hunting urges. You could also try playing with your cat outdoors to distract them from hunting or alternatively keeping them indoors during these times. Although be aware some cats may cope with this restriction of their freedom better than others!*

🐾 ***Cats are more likely to hunt, kill and/or eat their prey when hungry:*** *A well-fed cat may be less motivated to go out looking for prey or at least to kill or consume their prey once caught. Providing your cat* *with small, regular meals (ideally in puzzle feeders) or letting them have free, constant access to dry food (because it doesn't go off quickly when left out) may help to keep hunting at bay.*

Your cat scored mostly C's – what does this mean?

When it comes to play, it's unlikely that it's right at the top of your cat's daily to-do list. However, they probably still enjoy a good session every now and then. Perhaps a little encouragement from you might be just what they need to coax out their playful side a little more, in which case the following advice may be useful. It's also a very good idea to ensure you indulge your cat in all their passions, not just play, so the advice on pages 167–70 may be extremely useful too.

Tips and advice

The following may involve a bit of trial and error on your part, as well as some patience until you find what works best for your cat. Observe your cat when you're trying out the following techniques. You can use the checklist on pages 162–3 to determine which elicit the most playful or predatory responses from your cat.

🐾 *Try using toys that have the same appearance and texture as real prey. You can also experiment with toys that look and feel like different types of prey (for example, insects, mice, birds, even reptiles or fish!), until you find the ones your cat likes best.*

🐾 *Try using wand toys that can be moved in rapid, short bursts (as described in the test on page 161) to mimic prey-like movements. Some cats might also really like to 'hunt' moving objects that are concealed somehow (for example, a toy moved under a rug or from behind a curtain), so experiment with this too.*

🐾 *When playing with your cat, allow them to both 'catch' and 'kill' the toys as this will allow them to unleash as much of their predatory arsenal as possible. It will also ensure your cat doesn't become frustrated by not being able to complete the final parts of their hunting sequence. For this reason, using laser pointers to play with cats is generally not thought to be a good idea, unless you chuck them a few treats or a small furry toy to 'catch' every so often.*

🐾 *Provide your cat with opportunities for both 'self-play' (toys that your cat plays with alone) as well as 'interactive play' (toys that you operate). Some cats may enjoy both types of play, while others may prefer one over the other.*

🐾 *Try using toys loaded with catnip or valerian, which may help to stimulate your cat's senses a little more.*

🐾 *Change toys and introduce new objects regularly. In the wild, each hunting attempt would be over pretty quickly so some cats may not be very motivated to pursue the same prey item (or toy) over and over again. Studies suggest that changing the shape and appearance of toys can increase the amount of time a cat will play with them in a single session. If something isn't doing it for your cat, it's better to stop quickly and change to something else than to risk annoying them by constantly dangling something in front of their face that they just aren't interested in.*

🐾 *Try playing with your cat when they're in the garden. Their senses may become more heightened and this could help to get them in the mood for some play.*

Your cat scored mostly D's and E's – what does this mean?

As you're no doubt already very aware, your cat is probably not the most playful or predatory of felines – quite the opposite, in fact. It may be that, due to their specific personality, they just aren't that way inclined. Perhaps your cat has a range of other hobbies that keep them equally entertained and active (such as gate crashing your game of Scrabble, sending tiles flying everywhere, or knocking things off the coffee table with their front paws). Or maybe they prefer the quieter life and are usually just content with a bit of pottering about or sunbathing. There are a few other explanations as to why your cat isn't behaving quite like their supreme predatory relatives. For example:

🐾 *Your cat may be feeling stressed or unhappy. If your cat is frequently anxious or uncomfortable around the house, they are likely to want to prioritise their safety and security over the non-essentials such as play and exploration.*

🐾 *Your cat could be ill or in pain. A poorly or pained cat is unlikely to be a playful one. If your cat is usually up for a play session but you see a sudden decline in their interest, this could be due to deteriorating health.*

🐾 *Your cat may just be getting on a bit. As cats age, they naturally start to slow down (just like we do!). Domestic cats tend to live a lot longer than their wild counterparts and with this increased longevity comes a range of age-related diseases and illnesses. For example, arthritis is very common in older cats (usually from the age of ten onwards) and may start* to cause stiffness or pain when they move, meaning their desire to play dwindles.

🐾 *Your cat might just need a bit more encouragement or have more specialist requirements than the average cat; they may need a specific kind of toy to play with, in the right way.*

🐾 *It could be that your cat simply gets their kicks in other ways, preferring a range of other activities, such as exploring in their garden or tormenting the dog.*

🐾 *The breed of your cat may make it difficult for them to play a lot. Recent studies suggest that cats with extreme facial features, including a very flat, round-looking face with a short nose (a condition known as 'brachycephalism'), may struggle to breathe normally. This could mean that, while your cat still has the urges to play and explore, they get out of breath quickly and aren't able to do as much as they would like.*

🐾 *Your cat may not be that comfortable around you or other people. If you found that your cat doesn't really think that much of humans (see quiz on pages 6–35), it's possible that they simply don't feel at ease enough to unleash their predatory, playful ways when you're around.*

Tips and advice

Use the above information to try to determine the most likely reason for your cat's lack of playfulness and consider whether there's anything that might be useful for you to do. For example, if you're worried your cat might be stressed, you can take the quiz on pages 181–222 to learn more about which signs you should be looking out for and what you can do to help. Painful conditions such as arthritis can potentially be managed with pain relief, which might help to ramp up your cat's activity levels once more. If your cat can't be coaxed to play, even when you try making play time as exciting as possible for them, it's worth exploring other ways to keep them mentally and physically stimulated (see the advice sections on pages 167–70 for what to try). For cats that aren't that comfortable around people in general, access to a stimulating outdoor space may be crucial in providing them with the right environment to satisfy their predatory/playful nature.

🐾
Science corner

In the wild, cats will spend a large portion of their day searching and investigating their environment, looking for potential prey opportunities. Indeed, free-living cats can spend around 50 per cent of their time partaking in this activity, using all of their expertly attuned senses to help them.

Your cat's ears are basically two small, furry satellites, which are able to pinpoint the precise location of prey, based on sound alone. Cats have an exceptional hearing range and are even able to detect the ultrasonic noises made by mice and rats.

Your cat's eyes are also specially adapted to work well in low-light conditions (for example, at dusk and dawn), which is when their preferred prey is likely to be most active. Cat's eyes generally work best over longer distances, which means when prey is close by, their whiskers turn into tiny sensing probes, which better detect their position.

Cats may also use their sense of smell to locate burrows, based on the trails of urine left behind by the rodents coming in and out of them.

Finally, cat's canines are even equipped with special sensors so that they can determine exactly where to sink their teeth into their prey, ensuring they deliver the perfect 'kill bite'. All sounds pretty impressive, right? No wonder our well-fed felines are still so keen on the whole search and destroy thing.

SECTION 4:
A HAPPY CAT

In this section

How happy is your cat?

How well does your cat cope with change?

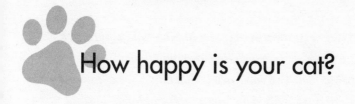

How happy is your cat?

Every responsible cat parent will obviously want their cat to be as happy and contented as possible. Good cat wellbeing is one of the most crucial ingredients in your harmonious cat–human relationship. A stressed, miserable or poorly cat does not make for a good furry companion. Just like with humans, the wellbeing of your cat will depend on a range of factors including:

🐾 *Their personality: Your cat's personality affects how they see the world, what they enjoy and what they are able to cope with. For example, a confident, laid-back, friendly cat may enjoy living closely alongside humans the most. They also tend to be able to cope much better with all the challenges domestic living brings than an anxious, highly strung or unfriendly cat who may be more likely to struggle.*

🐾 *Their previous experiences: For example, a cat that has experienced a stressful house move in their past may be more sensitive and become more anxious when you start moving large boxes around.*

🐾 ***Their environment:*** *Having the right environment for your cat is crucial in ensuring all their needs are being met. The basic needs that cats have are all very similar, though, depending on the individual, some may be more of a priority than others. For example, a very anxious cat might prioritise their safety more than a bold, confident cat, who might be more interested in exploration and thrill seeking!*

🐾 ***Their physical health:*** *If your cat is unwell or in pain, this can cause them to feel quite uncomfortable or a bit miserable. It may also reduce the amount of pleasure they are able to experience from their environment.*

🐾 ***Their mental state:*** *The cat's mental state will ultimately control how the cat feels about their situation. This is the most crucial aspect when it comes to your cat's overall level of wellbeing.*

To have good wellbeing, cats need to experience lots of pleasure and positive emotions, but also experience no (or very few) negative emotions and distress. Just as we all respond a little differently to stress, so do cats. The way your cat expresses how they're feeling will largely be influenced by what's causing them problems as well as any underlying health issues and their personality. In general, early signs of compromised wellbeing in cats can be easily missed. It's thought that this is due to the influence of the cat's wild relatives who are probably also a bit cryptic when it comes to showing signs of pain or ill health. Their stoic nature likely gives them an advantage because it helps them avoid looking like an easy target to predators or other wildcats wanting to muscle in on their territory. While some pet cats can be extremely vocal about how they're feeling, others may be much more introverted and hardly utter a meow about it.

The following quiz has been designed with these variables in mind and should help you to better understand what to look out for (including the more subtle signs), in order to gauge how your cat is generally faring. If you're ever in any doubt as to whether your cat might be unwell or suffering, a trip to the vets is always recommended; perhaps then followed up by a visit from a suitably qualified cat behaviour counsellor.

Signs of relaxation, contentedness or positive excitement: have you recently observed any of the following behaviours in your cat? (tick all that apply)

☐ A relaxed posture with no obvious tension in the body

☐ Resting on their side, exposing their sacred tummy area

☐ Curled up in a deep, peaceful sleep, even when they know you might be spying on them

☐ Tail held upright, raised to attention or gently waving from side to side in the air, as if plucking at an invisible harp

☐ A relaxed facial expression, ears facing forwards; it's almost as if they're smiling

☐ Eyes gently closed as if appreciating a beautiful piece of music

☐ Alert and interested in their environment, but not tense or uncomfortable. Their eyes may be round, but their ears should be pricked and generally pointed forwards

How often have you noticed any of these signs?

A. Pretty much all of the time; your cat seems to enjoy living with you!

B. Quite often

C. Occasionally, particularly when the house is calm and peaceful

D. Rarely

E. Never

Signs of tension, anxiety or fear: have you recently observed your cat doing any of the following? (tick all that apply)

☐ Blinking, shaking their head or body or licking their nose; brain reset is being attempted

☐ Suddenly deciding they are extremely dirty and launching into a short, frantic grooming session

☐ Suddenly going a bit still, doing their best statue impression

☐ Performing an exaggerated blink, perhaps also licking their nose or seeming to 'gulp' or do an obvious swallow

☐ Looking on edge and jumpy, easily startling at any sudden noises or movements

☐ All four feet firmly planted on the floor as if they're ready to ping off at a moment's notice

☐ Trying to hide, get up high or dart from one room to another when disturbed or startled

☐ A tense, hunched posture, all limbs pressed to their body, head pulled in as if they no longer have a neck

☐ Head turned away to one side or lowered to the ground

☐ Taking on a defensive posture, leaning back with front paws kept free, ready to swipe if necessary

☐ Hissing or swiping defensively

☐ A tense face and very wide, rounded eyes; huge pupils like two black saucers

☐ Ears rotated backwards a little and/or flattened downwards

☐ Ears pressed flat against their head as if they suddenly vanished

☐ A 'puffed up' tail, held either straight up or in a curve, their back arched (think about the classic 'Halloween cat')

☐ Moonwalking or walking sideways while in 'Halloween cat' mode

How often have you noticed any of these signs?

A. Never

B. Rarely

C. Occasionally, particularly when there are lots of stressful things going on at home

D. Often

E. Pretty much all of the time

Signs of annoyance or frustration: have you recently observed your cat doing any of the following? (tick all that apply)

☐ Meowing excessively

☐ Appearing restless or agitated

☐ Pacing repeatedly or performing other repetitive behaviours while indoors

☐ Skin that twitches or ripples as if someone's just walked over their grave; their fur might also look slightly puffed up

☐ Scratching excessively on the furniture or carpet

☐ Slightly narrowed eyes; their pupils may be small

☐ Tension in the face; whiskers may be splayed forwards

☐ Ears that rotate towards the back of their head

☐ A tail held at 'half mast'; it might also take on the appearance of an angry snake, swishing furiously from side to side or thumping up and down

☐ A tense posture, weight held forwards

☐ Behaving aggressively (i.e. growling, yowling, hissing, biting, swiping, attacking) towards you, other family members or visitors

☐ Suddenly attacking people, seemingly for no reason

☐ Behaving aggressively towards other pets in the home

How often have you noticed any of these signs?

A. Never

B. Rarely

C. Occasionally, particularly when there are lots of stressful things going on at home

D. Often

E. Pretty much all of the time

How many of the following activities does your cat enjoy?

Dinner time, being stroked, hanging out with their humans, greeting house guests, exploring and sunbathing in the garden, hunting and playing with toys, snoozing in warm places

A. All of them

B. Most of them

C. Some of them

D. A few of them, occasionally

E. None of them

Your cat gets worried, tense or anxious about:

A. Nothing, except if I might run out of their favourite treats

B. Only the obvious stuff like the vacuum cleaner, small noisy children, dogs, etc.

C. Any commotion and disturbance going on around the house

D. Most things; it's as if they're on high alert

E. Absolutely everything; it's almost as if they're afraid of their own shadow

Your cat gets annoyed or frustrated about:

A. Your cat's far too 'zen' to get annoyed

B. Not much, except perhaps if they really want to go outside but the cat flap's stuck in the closed position

C. A few things, especially when there's a lot of change going on around them or if you forget about feeding or cuddle time

D. Lots of things, especially when you disappoint them by forgetting *your* place in *their* household

E. Pretty much everything

Physical signs of stress: have you ever observed any of the following in your cat? (tick all that apply)

☐ Diarrhoea

☐ Vomiting

☐ Pica (eating of non-food items, such as cat litter, string or wool)

☐ Poor appetite and eating less than usual

☐ Eating or drinking more than usual

☐ Suddenly gaining or losing weight

☐ Excessive grooming or not grooming enough

☐ Not going to the toilet as regularly as usual (urine and/ or faeces)

☐ Toileting indoors, outside of the litter tray (for example, behind the sofa, under the bed or on the bed)

☐ Urine spraying on furniture and other items around the house

☐ A runny nose and eyes (i.e. cat flu)

☐ Frequent squatting and straining to pass urine, pain when urinating or urine with blood in it (i.e. cystitis)

☐ Taking a long time to recover from illness or their underlying conditions seem to get worse or flare up (i.e. they have a weakened immune system)

How often have you noticed any of these signs?

A. Never

B. Once or twice, but it resolves quickly

C. Occasionally, particularly when there are lots of stressful things going on at home

D. Often

E. Pretty much all the time

Your cat's current body type is:

A. Athletic, with a clear waist, visible behind the hips and minimal paunch

B. Slim, but with a few slightly squishy bits
   OR: Extremely toned with an obvious waist

C. A bit on the paunchy side: waist not obvious and ribs hidden under a generous layer of fat
   OR: Very lean: obvious waist and ribs clearly felt

D. Like a couch potato: no waist or ribs to speak of and a large paunch
   OR: Like an extreme dieter: ribs visible, minimal muscle mass and tummy tucked in

E. Like a furry beach ball when viewed from above: belly very large and distended
   OR: Extremely thin and bony looking: ribs clearly protruding on short-haired cats

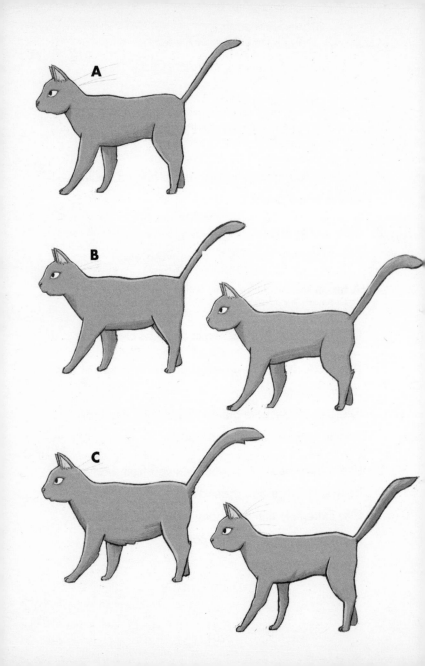

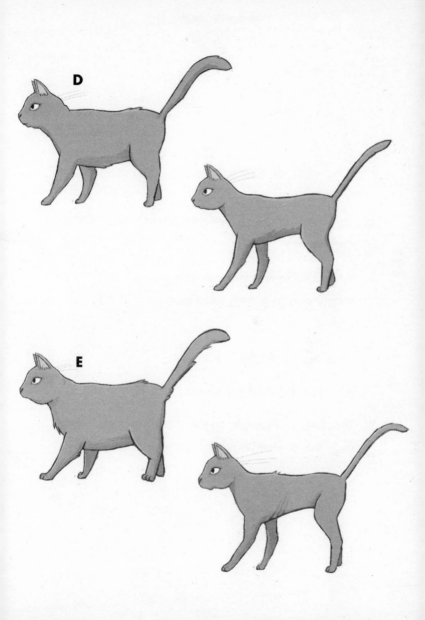

Your cat's current coat is:

A. Shampoo-commercial quality: smooth, silky, shiny and healthy

B. Pretty healthy-looking with only the very occasional scruffy part (e.g. mat, bald spot, bit of dandruff, grease, etc.)

C. Usually a bit scruffy in places

D. Always a bit scruffy in places

E. The 'before' example on the shampoo commercial (e.g. lots of mats, bald spots, dandruff or grease)

Behavioural signs of stress: have you recently observed any of the following in your cat? (tick all that apply)

☐ Any noticeable changes in their usual behaviour patterns or routines

☐ Avoiding being inside the house at certain times of the day (e.g. when it's busiest)

☐ Avoiding certain rooms or areas of the house at particular times

☐ A reluctance to come into the house or a reluctance to go outside

☐ Frequent hiding

☐ Becoming more responsive to things going on around them (for example, they are more jumpy or easily startled, perhaps resting and sleeping less than usual too)

☐ Becoming unresponsive to things going on around them (for example, they are less jumpy or easily startled than usual)

☐ A decreased interest in things that they usually enjoy, such as treats, play and attention

☐ Appearing quiet, withdrawn or lethargic, perhaps sleeping more than usual

☐ An increased dependency on you or other family members; they constantly want to interact with you or get your attention

☐ Withdrawal from you or other family members; they are no longer interested in interacting

How often have you noticed any of these signs?

A. Never

B. Rarely

C. Occasionally, especially when there are lots of stressful things going on at home

D. Often

E. Pretty much all of the time

Behavioural signs of pain or general illness: have you recently observed any of the following in your cat? (tick all that apply)

☐ Reduced or increased eating and/or drinking

☐ Rapid weight loss or weight gain

☐ Difficulty or pain when toileting (urine and/or faeces)

☐ Sickness and/or diarrhoea

☐ Certain parts of their body becoming sensitive (i.e. your cat might shout at you or give you a swipe or nibble if you try to touch those areas)

☐ A general reduction in grooming or grooming one part of their body excessively

☐ Lameness

☐ A reduction in their movement and general activity levels

☐ Avoiding strenuous activities such as jumping up

☐ Hiding away and general avoidance of people/other animals

☐ Moodiness or irritability

☐ Lethargic, depressed or withdrawn, reduced interested in things they used to enjoy

☐ Frequent, unpleasant or urgent-sounding meows, groaning, hissing, growling, yowling

☐ Sudden changes in posture, including more tension, crouching and hunching, lowering of the head and gaze

☐ Ears pressed down the sides of their head, tension around the nose, tense 'squinted' eyes, cheeks and whiskers appearing tense or compressed

How many of these signs have you noticed?

A. Definitely none of them

B. Pretty sure none of them

C. One of them

D. Two of them

E. More than two of them

Which of these scales best reflects your cat's experiences?

Positive experiences: enjoyment, excitement, relaxation, contentment, play, exploration

Negative experiences: fear, anxiety, frustration, anger, pain, discomfort, stress, distress

 A. Your cat has **a lot more** positive than negative experiences

 B. Your cat has **more** positive than negative experiences

 C. Your cat has **equal** amounts of positive and negative experiences

D. Your cat has **more** negative than positive experiences (although there are probably things you can do to help improve this)

E. Your cat has **a lot more** negative than positive experiences (and you're not sure if there's anything you can do to help them)

Interpret your cat's score

Your cat scored mostly A's and B's – what does this mean?

All signs suggest your precious cat pal is doing pretty great right now. He or she is likely to have a good level of general wellbeing and probably gets of lot of joy out of life. Your cat's basic needs are likely to have been sufficiently met. However, if there's one thing we know about our enigmatic felines, it's that sometimes things can go south very quickly. As we know it can often be quite hard to spot some of the subtle, early signs of stress or pain. It's therefore important to keep a close eye on your cat, looking out for any potential changes in their health, appearance or behaviour. This is especially important when things are a little busier in the home than usual or there are lots of changes taking place.

Your cat scored mostly C's – what does this mean?

Your cat is in a state of balance where the good and bad they experience are about equal. There's certainly scope to improve their wellbeing, ideally so that the good bits outweigh the bad as much as possible. Your cat might be quite a sensitive soul and simply need a bit more support from you to ensure their needs are being properly met. They just might not be well-suited to their current living arrangements, which are causing them stress. In this case, some big changes might be necessary in order to improve things for your cat.

If your cat is not the happiest, you might also find that this impacts on the relationship you have with them. Studies have shown that stress and illness can have a huge influence on an animals' personality and how they behave around humans. Often, the more miserable or in pain your cat is, the less likely they are to want to hang out with you and be smoochy. To understand a bit more about the basic needs of cats, their priorities and how to meet them, see the advice section opposite. The needs numbered 2–4 may be the ones to particularly focus on. A trip to the vets to rule out any underlying medical problems is always a good idea too, potentially followed up by a visit from a suitably qualified cat behaviour counsellor.

Your cat scored mostly D's and E's – what does this mean?

All signs suggest that there's something up with your furry little friend. They're clearly not the happiest of cats and will certainly need your help if things are going to improve. They are likely to find life pretty challenging, although the reasons behind this may vary depending on the cat in question. What all 'D' and 'E' cats will have in common, though, is that some or perhaps all of their basic needs are not being met, therefore trying to better accommodate these should be the primary focus. If you feel that your cat's needs simply cannot be sufficiently met in their current environment, then relocating them to a more suitable one may be the kindest thing to do. To learn more about your cat's needs, their priorities and how to potentially meet them, see the advice section below. The needs numbered 1–3 may be the ones to particularly focus on right now. A trip to the vets to rule out any underlying medical problems is always a good idea too, potentially followed up by a visit from a suitably qualified cat behaviour counsellor.

Tips and advice for all cats

A great way to provide your cat with a good level of wellbeing is to ensure that all of their basic needs are being met and to understand which might be of highest priority for them, at any given time. A useful way to approach this is to see your cat's needs as forming a pyramid or hierarchy with the most important or fundamental needs at the bottom. When the lowest need is sufficiently met, the need above then becomes the priority for the cat, and so on, moving up to the top. For domestic pet cats, their needs are likely to focus around four core areas; all of which are important in ensuring they stay happy and healthy. Where your cat currently 'sits' on the pyramid will depend on both their personality and current level of wellbeing, although cats with poorer wellbeing are more likely to sit somewhere near the bottom.

Positive stimulation

The cat has regular access to things around them, which keep them happy and entertained. For example: an enriching outdoor and indoor environment, toys, puzzle feeders, things to climb on and explore. For friendly cats: attention from humans. For cats bonded to other animals: interactions with them too.

A predictable and stable environment

The cat's daily routine is sufficiently predictable, and their environment is calm and stable. He or she can anticipate when and how things happen, and they have a sense on control over their life.

Personal safety and secure access to resources

The cat can withdraw from situations they find frightening or unpleasant. He or she feels that they have safe access to all their important resources (such as food and water, litter trays, hiding spots, places to get up high, quiet places for sleeping/resting, a garden, toys, scratching posts, human attention).

Basic physical functions

The cat has good quality food and fresh water provided daily, and a comfortable environment for resting and sleeping within. He or she can pass faeces and urine comfortably and has good physical health with no pain, injury or disease.

Need 1 – Basic physical functions

The most basic needs are for your cat to have good nutrition, a comfortable environment, be able to pass faeces and urine comfortably, be in good physical health and free from pain, injury and disease. If you're concerned that any of these are missing for your cat, it's a great idea to:

🐾 *Take them to the vets for a check up.*

🐾 *If they are currently being treated for a medical condition, make sure you keep an eye on how they're generally faring to ensure the treatment is actually helping to improve their condition.*

🐾 *Check they have daily access to a good quality, complete cat food and fresh drinking water. Some cats might prefer wet or dry food or a combination, and most cats enjoy variety in their diet (e.g. different flavours, textures, shapes and sizes of food). Many cats will be put off by stale food, a dirty cat bowl or water that's been left out for some time. Some cats might prefer rain water, drinking from a cat water fountain or a dripping tap.*

🐾 *Check they have warm places to rest and sleep. Cat's body temperatures are a bit higher than ours (about 38–39° Celsius compared to our 36–37). This means they can tolerate, and will generally prefer, slightly higher temperatures to us. Very young, old, small or ill cats, or those without fur, will especially appreciate being provided with a constant source of warmth. A special heated pet blanket can be a great idea, particularly in the winter and at times of the day when the temperature in the house falls (e.g. overnight).*

❧ *Cats will also sleep better when they are on a soft, comfortable surface, so provide lots of warm, fleecy blankets and beds for them to snooze on. Again, this is especially important for old, frail cats or those that are unwell or in pain.*

Need 2 – Personal safety and secure access to resources

Once your cat's basic physical functions are sufficiently met, the next priority should be for them to feel safe and to have secure access to all of their important resources (e.g. food and water bowls, beds, places they can hide and get up high, litter trays, scratching posts, toys, cat flaps, attention from you, etc.). If you are concerned that this may not be the case for your cat, it's a great idea to do the following:

🐾 *Ensure your cat is easily able to avoid the things they find scary or that make them feel uncomfortable. Don't be tempted to restrain them or stop them from being able to make a speedy getaway if they ever want to. Provide them with lots of places where they can hide and get up high.*

🐾 *Ensure your cat doesn't feel too exposed or under threat when they want to access their resources (for example, they should feel calm and safe when using their cat flap, snacking at the food bowl or using their litter tray). You can help by choosing carefully where you place these things; avoid busy parts of the house, where the cat might suddenly feel ambushed by humans (especially young children) or other animals.*

🐾 *You can also try placing additional hiding and perching places (e.g. cardboard boxes, cat tunnels, cat trees, chairs, etc.) near to your cat's important resources, so they know there's always a safety option nearby.*

Need 3 – A predictable and stable environment:

Once your cat feels safe and secure, the next priority should be to ensure their daily routine feels sufficiently predictable and that their environment is calm and stable. Your cat needs to feel that they can anticipate when and how things happen around them and that they have a sense of control over their life. If you're concerned that your cat may need more support in this area, it's a great idea to try some of the following:

🐾 *Make sure your cat has constant, predictable access to all of their important resources.*

🐾 *Notice if your cat likes to sleep, go outside, be in specific rooms, eat, play or have attention at certain times of the day. This will help you to get a good sense of their preferred daily routines so that you can avoid disturbing them as much as possible.*

🐾 *If your cat goes outside and you don't already have one, try installing a (microchip-operated) cat flap and let your cat come and go as they please at times they choose rather than having to open the door to let them in or out. This type of cat flap is also the best for stopping intruder cats from entering the home, which can be a major source of stress for cats.*

🐾 *Try feeding your cat at the same time each day in the same (quiet/safe) location.*

🐾 *If your cat craves attention, try putting aside a bit of quality time for them at the same time(s) each day.*

🐾 *If your cat is very playful/predatory, try putting aside a bit of quality play time at the same time(s) each day.*

🐾 *Work out your cat's preferred 'stroking protocol' (see quiz 36–59) and stick to this each time you both interact.*

🐾 *Try to keep household disturbances (e.g. vacuuming, cleaning, playing loud music) to set periods of time each day or set days of the week if possible, so that your cat can anticipate when these things are likely to happen and then go where they feel safest.*

🐾 *If you're planning to do lots of redecorating or construction work around the house, try limiting your cat's exposure to this by temporarily separating off a quiet part of the house for them to be in. Ensure that, wherever you put your cat, you provide them with all of their usual resources. Alternatively, you could take your cat to stay at a friend's house or a good cattery for a little while (if you think they might cope well with this). Try to choose a friend who doesn't have young children or other animals and has a quiet home with lots of places for your cat to hide.*

Need 4 – Positive Stimulation:

If all your other cat's needs are sufficiently met, they will prioritise having regular access to things around them that help keep them stimulated and entertained. Depending on their personality, some cats may prefer certain sources of stimulation over others, although the usual ones include:

- 🐾 *An enriching outdoor space (see the advice section on pages 167–9 for more info).*

- 🐾 *Toys, puzzle feeders, things to climb on and explore inside (see advice section on pages 169–70 for more info).*

- 🐾 *For friendly cats, play and attention from humans (see the quiz on pages 36–59 to learn more about how your cat likes to be stroked and pages 173–5 for tips on how to play with your cat).*

- 🐾 *For cats bonded to other animals, play and interactions with them.*

Science corner

What does it mean when cats blink at us?
Are they telling us they're happy?

It's a common belief that when cats look at us and perform of sort of 'slow blink', they're in effect blowing us a kiss. However, as with most things feline, the truth is probably a little more complicated. Cats may actually blink at us, as well as other animals, in a range of different scenarios – sometimes when they are happy and contented, but other times when they are feeling very uncomfortable or distressed. Indeed, recent evidence suggests that cats may blink at humans when they are feeling anxious or afraid of them. While science can't yet tell us exactly why cats blink in these different situations, or what it means, it might be that the purpose of blinking is similar. By blinking, the cat is breaking eye contact with us, rather than continually staring, so the cat may be trying to signal that they are not a 'threat' to us, to avoid possible conflict. So, in theory, a relaxed, friendly cat may blink for the same reason that a fearful distressed cat does – in both cases they are trying to say 'I don't intend to cause any trouble'. Therefore, we shouldn't always assume that a cat that's slow blinking is saying they are happy or want to be friends – they might actually be feeling quite the opposite. If we want to under-stand our furry friends better, it's important to try to work out why they might want to signal this – is it because they feel at ease and are happy to be around us? Is it because they feel frightened and are worried we might attack them? Or do they just feel a little uncomfortable, and want to diffuse possible tension? Paying close attention to the cat's body language and facial expression while they are blinking will help to answer these questions. For more information on the sorts of other behaviours to look out for, see pages 100–1 and 187–9.

How does your cat cope with change?

As we know, our pet cats have a very different lifestyle to that of their closest wild relatives. The Near Eastern wildcat lives and hunts alone, goes where it wants, when it wants, and has its own carefully selected and defended territory. In stark contrast to this, we pretty much decide and control all of these aspects for our pets. We choose who they live with, how big their territory is and what they have access to and when.

Most cats certainly appreciate all that we provide them with, although they still remain creatures of habit who are very sensitive to their surroundings, craving a sense of security and control. Various events in our lives can cause us stress and we may often underestimate the effect these also tend to have on our furry companions. Events such as a new addition to the household (whether this be two- or four-legged), a house move or a cat's humans going away on holiday are just a few of the things that can make a cat feel as if they've had the rug pulled from under them. Their reactions to these changes and how much of them they can cope with will be influenced by their underlying personality. In addition to this, how we manage our cats when facing these challenges can greatly impact on their coping potential. Take the following quiz to find out how well your cat is likely to fare during various life upheavals and what you can do to coach them through it.

You go away on holiday for two weeks and have a pet sitter looking after your cat. How is your cat?

A. Having a great time, staying up late and enjoying all the extra treats!

B. Adjusting well to the slightly altered feeding schedule and stroking protocols

C. A bit agitated, seemingly not too happy about all the disruptions to their routine

D. Totally unable to relax and accept this new intruder

E. The cat sitter will be lucky to catch more than a few glimpses of your cat

You're in bed for the week with the flu. Does your cat:

A. Rejoice at the sheer amount of daily cuddling opportunities that await

B. Quite like the idea of having food and attention on tap

C. Feel OK about it, as long as you don't disturb their nap times

D. Prefer you make a speedy recovery so you stop ruining their week

E. Look for somewhere else to live

You arrive home from work a little earlier than usual. Does your cat?

A. Remain stretched, flat-out, on the comfiest part on your bed

B. Become inquisitive, coming to see what's going on

C. Continue to mind their own business, hoping you do the same

D. Get a little agitated, clearly worried by this unexpected event

E. Enter into full-on panic mode, looking for the nearest hiding place

You find yourself coming home from work late and generally being around the house less than usual. How does your cat greet you when you arrive home?

A. Your cat is happy to break off from whatever they were doing to come and greet you

B. Your cat quickly trots over, tail up, chirrups or meows and gives you a few head rubs

C. Your cat is already waiting impatiently by the door, ready to demand things

D. There's a lot of meowing, pawing, climbing all over you and following you around

E. They're avoiding you, as per usual

You've recently broken up with
your partner whom your cat
adored. How is your cat?

A. Pretty happy and relaxed as long as food and
   attention continue to arrive on schedule

B. Looking a little confused at times but happy for the
   extra attention they're getting from you

C. Sometimes restless and a bit more meowy than usual

D. Generally restless, anxious or agitated

E. Seemingly withdrawn or lethargic

You're trying to write a difficult email and need to concentrate, but your cat wants attention. What do they do?

A. Wait patiently nearby, keeping a close eye out for any signs that you might be available

B. Give you a gentle cheek rub or two and emit a couple of hopeful 'chirrup' or meow sounds

C. Meow at you with great urgency and nuzzle you vigorously, using their annoying furry body to block your view

D. Frantically paw at you, shout at you, climb on you, bite you – whatever works

E. This would never happen – your cat hates it when you give them attention

You're on the phone, catching up with an old friend, and you've missed your cat's usual feeding time. Have they:

A. Hardly noticed; they're enjoying the additional lap time they get while you chat

B. Been pretty patient so far, except for the occasional meow and rubbing around your legs

C. Been crouching nearby, giving you the odd evil every now and then

D. Been shouting at you constantly for the past ten minutes

E. Been anxiously waiting at a safe distance until you've put the food down and cleared off

You've just placed some freshly ironed clothes on your bed. You notice your cat's about to jump up and make themselves comfortable, so decide to shut them out of the bedroom. Does your cat:

A. Accept this banishing gracefully and saunter over to the food bowl

B. Seem a little disappointed by this sudden denial of entry, but wait patiently until access is restored

C. Look confused or slightly irritated

D. Meow their head off and paw at the door until you give in and open it for them

E. Not care in the slightest; the bedroom is not a fun place to be anyway (because that's where you usually are)

It's the first day for you and your cat in your new house. What's your cat doing?

A. Strutting around as if they own the place, exploring everything

B. Acting a little cautious to begin with, but seemingly keen to check out their new surroundings; there is lots of sniffing and rubbing of objects going on

C. Looking quite alert and on edge, holding their body low to the ground, trying to figure out all the entry and exit points

D. Pressed up in the back of the cat carrier, refusing to come out

E. You think they made a dash for the nearest small, dark space and that's where they'll be for at least a week

You get inspired by one of those home decluttering TV programmes and decide it's time to take action; you're moving furniture and boxes around all day. What's your cat doing?

A. 'Helping' you by inspecting each box carefully and making sure they fit inside it

B. Inquisitively checking out the new furniture locations

C. Looking a bit perturbed – I liked things as they were, human!

D. Steering clear of all commotion until it's over

E. You have no idea, but you're unlikely to see them in the next 24 hours

You're decorating for a few weeks;
it's noisy, there's paint everywhere and
you need to keep your cat out of several
rooms of the house, which they usually
spend time in. Does your cat:

A. Carry on as usual – there's still plenty to do and
    they're glad you finally got rid of that terrible
    brown wallpaper

B. Seem a little confused by the relocation of their things,
    but adjust well

C. Seem a little on edge, invest a great deal of time
    sniffing everything, occasionally sit outside the
    closed doors

D. Seem agitated, frequently pace, meow and scratch at
    the various doors

E. Seem tense, hunched and generally uncomfortable

Interpret your cat's score

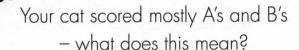

Your cat scored mostly A's and B's – what does this mean?

Your cat is probably on the laid-back side, able to take quite a lot in their stride. He or she may generally feel quite at ease and comfortable in their environment, dealing with the upheaval or commotion well. However, even the coolest of cats still wants to feel as if they've got a handle on things, so it's important to make sure they are managed with this in mind during any major life events. See the section below for some useful tips and advice and be sure to keep a close eye on them to make sure they're still coping well.

Your cat scored mostly C's – what does this mean?

Your cat is probably a delicate soul. They may tend to be quite sensitive to change and disruption, sometimes becoming bothered by even the smallest of things. They are probably the kind of cat that enjoys a specific daily routine, something which will help them to feel a little more in control of their surroundings. They will appreciate the feeling that they have safe, predictable access to all the things they value in life, be this food, good hiding spots, access to the garden, somewhere quiet to hide or even attention from you. Especially when it comes to the big stuff going on around them, your cat is likely to find additional support invaluable. See the section overleaf for some useful tips and advice.

Your cat scored mostly D's and E's – what does this mean?

Just like 'C' cats, your cat is likely to be very sensitive or reactive to the world around them. They might already be finding life a bit on the challenging side, seemingly even without anything very major going on. They may be easily worried by even the smallest changes that take place, perhaps generally not feeling very in control of anything. The reasons behind this can be varied and complex, although these are a few of the common ones:

🐾 *Your cat may be a bit of a control freak or quite inflexible. They can become easily annoyed or frustrated when the reality of a situation doesn't quite meet their expectations. They may then struggle to adjust or to feel as if they have a handle on things.*

🐾 *Your cat has an anxious or fearful personality, becoming easily worried when life is less predictable than they need it to be. This anxiety may extend to include humans, other animals or just be in relation to their physical surroundings. Again, such cats are likely to struggle to feel as if they are in control.*

🐾 *Your cat may be experiencing stress caused by other factors (such as conflict with other cats in the household/neighbourhood or an underlying medical condition), which makes it harder for them to deal with other things going on around them.*

🐾 *Your cat's current lifestyle isn't able to meet enough of their basic needs. Cats have several fundamental requirements in order to have good wellbeing.*

Tips and advice for all cats

One of the main issues associated with any type of negative change affecting your cat is the potential uncertainty that goes with it. Whether this change is associated with the disappearance of something positive in their life (such as access to their favourite person), or the presence of something negative (for example, noise and disturbance), it's often the uncertainty and lack of control this creates for your cat that is the worst part.

The key principles of supporting your cat through various life upheavals focus on ensuring that all their basic needs are being consistently met. See the advice section on pages 213–20 and read on to learn more about these basic needs. For cats experiencing a period of change in their environment, it's most likely that their needs for 'personal safety' (need 2) and 'predictability' (need 3) start to feel a little under threat. These are likely to be the top priority for your cat, so finding ways to meet these, in spite of whatever else is going on around you both, is the key.

🐾 ***Personal safety:*** *If cats feel that their safety is being threatened, their instincts are to escape or hide. If they can't do either of these things, then they may have to resort to violence. A change of environment, loud noises and disturbances can all cause your cat anxiety, so ensure that they always have a few quiet places (or somewhere up high) they can retreat to and hide if they feel unsafe. If your cat feels as if they have to run a gauntlet each time they want some food, to use their cat flap or litter tray, for example, this can also cause them a great deal of stress. Therefore, try to place these items in locations that are quiet and that your cat can easily get to without feeling too exposed. Placing additional* *hiding and perching places about the house (for example, cardboard boxes, cat tunnels, cat trees and chairs) near to your cat's food bowl or litter tray can help them to feel safer when accessing these things. If you're moving house, its ideal to initially keep your cat (along with all their important belongings) in one quiet room in the new place. When they appear more settled, you can let them explore the rest of their new digs, but again think carefully about where you place their resources and where might be good to install some cat 'safe houses'.*

🐾 ***Predictability:*** *Even if cats don't feel as if they're under threat, they often still crave a sense of order to their lives. Some cats will need this sense of predictability more than others and some may need it only in relation to certain things around them, so it's important be aware of your cat's individual preferences and priorities. For example, some cats may become agitated when their humans are suddenly in the house more than usual, while others may become agitated when they're away more often. Some cats may feel on edge if the furniture is moved around, while other cats may be curious and keen to investigate. Even when there's a lot of change* *going on for you both, either try to stick to the usual routines your cat is used to or start to create more of a daily routine for them.*

SECTION 5: CAT PARENTING

In this section

Are you ready to be a cat parent?

What kind of cat parent are you?
(And what cat is right for you?)

Whether you're new to the whole cat parenting thing, you already have a cat or you've had furry companions in the past, there's always more to learn about these mysterious bundles of joy. While it's very easy to get a cat, the keeping them healthy and happy part is not always as straightforward as it might seem. If looked after well, many cats can live for up to around 20 years, which means that you and your furry companion might be together for quite some time. Good cat parenting is as much about understanding the needs of your cat (and being able to provide these), as it is about selecting the right cat for you and your home in the first place. If either of these things aren't quite there, the domestic feline harmony you've always dreamed about may be in jeopardy. Indeed, many of the behaviours that we may find undesirable in our cats (for example, house-soiling, aggressive behaviour towards us and other animals or generally avoiding us are most often caused by incompatibilities between the cat and their living situation. These undesirable behaviours are also some of the most common reasons for people to give their cats away or surrender them to a rehoming charity. However, in many cases, these problems can be avoided by making sure you choose the right cat for you to start with and by ensuring you can easily meet each other's needs. To help get you started, take the following quizzes to see how ready you are to be a cat parent and what kind of cat might be your perfect match.

Are you ready to be a cat parent?

You've already got a pretty full house (e.g. loads of humans, cats and other animals) and are about to redecorate. Although you quite like the idea of another cat, do you:

A. Decide that this probably isn't the right time and put things on hold until it quietens down a bit

B. Think about the type of cat that would be able to cope well in your chaotic household

C. Decide to go to the local rehoming centre tomorrow to see what's available

D. Start looking on the internet for kittens for sale

E. Go out and get one straight away – if it doesn't work out you can always take them back!

You're thinking about what type of cat you might like to adopt from a local rehoming centre. What are your selection criteria?

A. You're happy to consider any cats whose requirements match with you and your home

B. You'd prefer the cat that seemed most comfortable around you when you met

C. You're hoping for the sorriest, saddest-looking cat to rescue, even if you're not the best match

D. You want the kind of stunning super cat that the neighbours will be jealous of

E. You want whichever cat will look cutest on your Instagram

It's your cat's first day in their new home. How do you settle them in?

A. In their own private living quarters, furnished with cat beds, hiding places, cat trees, litter trays, food, water, toys and a scratching post

B. In a quiet room in the house with a hiding box, some food, water and a litter tray nearby

C. By giving them the run of the house, letting them go where they want

D. By leaving them in the cat carrier for a while, until they stop meowing

E. By throwing them in at the deep end, starting with the busiest part of the house

Where will your cat be able to go when they want some alone time?

A. One of about ten different locations dotted about the house, all resplendent with cat bed, hiding box or climbing tree

B. There will be several designated cat places around the house for them

C. There's one spot that's usually quiet in the house, so probably there

D. Things are a bit chaotic so wherever happens to be most quiet at the time – they won't really have specific places

E. They probably won't really get much alone time in the house

Where will you place your cat's resources (e.g. food and water bowls, beds and hiding places, litter trays, etc.)?

A. All in quiet parts of the house. Additionally, food, water bowls and litter trays will be placed a little separate from each other (no one wants to poo in their dining area!)

B. In places your cat can easily get to without being too disturbed in the process

C. Hidden away in a corner or utility room, out of sight because they smell bad

D. In the kitchen, next to the washing machine, all clumped together

E. They will probably just have a food bowl somewhere

How will you keep your cat entertained?

A. There will be toys, oh so many toys! (Also puzzle feeders, cat climbing trees, cat shelves, beds, tunnels and, of course, a garden filled with plants, a cat water fountain, a heated outdoor cat house, a cat hammock …)

B. Lots of play and attention if my cat wants it, plus access to a fun outdoor space

C. You'll give them some food and a few toys and leave them to it

D. Cats are independent so shouldn't need any help in this department

E. Isn't the cat supposed to entertain me?!

Your cat starts biting or swiping at you
when you're stroking them. Will you:

A. Try to understand why; are you handling them in the
   way that they actually like? Could they be stressed or
   in pain?

B. Give them a little break from stroking and then allow
   them to call the shots a bit more from now on

C. Keep on stroking them as usual, but try to anticipate
   when they're about to attack, then whip your hands
   away super fast

D. Return them – your cat is clearly faulty and not fit
   for purpose

E. Assume this is their personality and that they enjoy the
   little 'play fights' you have

Your cat has recently started weeing behind the sofa. Do you:

A. Understand that this could be caused by the cat feeling stressed or unwell. Perhaps there's also something they don't like about their usual toilet location (i.e. their litter tray or outside). You'll do whatever you can to sort this!

B. Keep an eye on them and potentially take them to the vets for an initial health check if the situation doesn't improve

C. Clean up the wee and block off their access to the sofa

D. Assume they are spiteful and just doing it to annoy you

E. Shout at them if you catch them doing it

An intruder cat is regularly coming
into your garden and you're worried
he might be bullying your cat. Do you:

A. Try to find out if this bully cat has any parents so you
can try to manage the situation

B. Keep an eye on your cat whenever they're outside
and chase that naughty feline away!

C. Make sure your cat isn't injured; if not, it's probably
nothing to worry about

D. As long as your cat doesn't start weeing or pooing in
the house, it's not really a problem

E. Do nothing – it's best if they just fight it out

Your cat has been a little bit
quiet recently and you think they
may have lost weight. Do you:

A. Call your vet straight away and get them booked in
   for a check up

B. Keep an eye on them for a few more days; if nothing
   improves then you'll call the vet

C. Try changing their food to see if that perks them up
   a bit

D. Try giving them a bit more attention – perhaps they
   just need a hug?

E. Do nothing – cats are independent creatures and are
   good at sorting themselves out!

Interpret your score

You scored mostly A's and B's – what does this mean?

Congratulations! You're going to make a fantastic cat parent! All signs suggest that when it comes to looking after your future feline, you'll put a lot of thought and effort into it, taking this great responsibility seriously. You're likely to be committed to meeting the basic needs of your cat, ensuring they are as happy and contented as possible. However, as responsible cat parents, we must never become complacent. The varied personalities of cats, coupled with their enigmatic nature, mean that it's important that we treat each cat as an individual and try to carefully work out their specific needs, likes and dislikes.

You scored mostly C's – what does this mean?

While your heart might certainly be in the right place, a little more careful consideration is probably necessary before you're totally ready to be a cat parent. No one starts out as a cat whisperer (and the best ones spend a LONG time studying!), so a bit of advance research to help understand your future furry cat child a little better is always a great idea.

You scored mostly D's and E's – what does this mean?

At least for now, being a cat parent probably isn't the right thing for you. All animals that are suited to live as pets have a set of basic needs or requirements. These needs are fundamental to ensuring that they have a good quality of life and, ultimately, it's our responsibility to ensure they are provided for. Domestic living can potentially be a bit challenging for cats at times, so it's important that we are there to provide them with the right kind of support when they need it.

Tips and advice for all scores

To understand more about the basic needs of cats, read the advice on pages 213–20. You can also learn more about their behaviour and how to manage them optimally, in a range of different situations, by studying the other advice sections throughout this book. In addition, there are lots of other good books and websites out there written by well-respected, suitably qualified cat professionals. All of these will certainly be useful in helping you to better get to grips with the feline spirt and what it needs to shine brightly.

What kind of cat parent are you? (And what kind of cat is right for you?)

You get home from work after a long, tiring day. How would you prefer your cat to greet you?

A. Like you've been gone for at least a year (and they've missed you a LOT)

B. Enthusiastically: they are keen to give you a little paw massage while they find out how your meetings went

C. However they feel most appropriate: perhaps some sniffing and a couple of cheek rubs – you probably smell a bit weird

D. A quick nod in your direction will suffice

E. You'd prefer they just carried on with whatever it was they were doing

How important are cat cuddles to you?

A. About as important as oxygen

B. You need to get your fix at least several times a day

C. You're grateful for them whenever your cat deems you worthy

D. You can take them or leave them

E. You're probably allergic to cats

You're working from home for the day.
Where would you prefer your cat to be?

A. On your desk, purring and nuzzling all over you

B. Sitting contentedly in your lap

C. Wherever they feel most comfortable

D. Off doing their own thing

E. Anywhere, as long as they don't pester you

What's your idea of the perfect cat–human relationship?

A. Having a furry cat child that loves you as much as you love them

B. A strong, mutually beneficial bond

C. For you to enjoy each other's company

D. One that's convenient for both of you

E. You give them food and then they eat it

It's 6.30am and you're snoozing,
but your cat thinks it's time you
got up and fed them. Do you:

A. Leap out of bed immediately and follow them into
the kitchen

B. Snooze for a little longer, then go and feed them

C. Stay in bed until you're ready to get up, but offer
them a bit of fuss in the meantime

D. Roll over and pretend you can't hear them

E. Remind yourself to shut them out of the bedroom
in future

Which three words would best describe your ideal cat?

A. Loving, needy, intense

B. Friendly, interactive, inquisitive

C. Amenable, laid-back, calm

D. Aloof, independent, self-sufficient

E. Avoidant, disinterested, quiet

Your cat seems to like
meowing at you. Do you:

A. Take great pleasure in this, meowing back

B. Usually reply with a few friendly words

C. Assume they're probably hungry or want attention

D. Tell them they're being annoying

E. Pretend you can't hear them

It's freezing outside and your
cat is spending more time
indoors than usual. Are you:

A. Thrilled at the thought of lots of cosy nights in,
    snuggling together

B. Pleased by the extra attention you'll get

C. Happy to provide them with more play and attention
    if they want it

D. OK about it as long as they don't pester you too much

E. A bit annoyed by all the extra cat hair on the sofa

Interpret your score

You scored mostly A's – what does this mean?

You're probably the kind of feline parent that really is after a small, furry cat child. You have a lot of love to give and you're looking for that special feline that's ready to take it all. You'd probably happily forego an exciting evening out with friends simply to hang out with your cat, lavishing them with endless cuddles and treats. While there's no doubt that you will invest a lot of love and enthusiasm into your role as a cat parent, what's crucial is that you choose the right kind of cat that's going to appreciate all you have to offer. When it comes to their level of friendliness towards humans, domestic cats can vary massively. While some special felines are super sociable love bugs, there are probably just as many cats that can't stand the sight of us and even more that quite like us, but don't enjoy being smothered. You're potentially going to have to do a little careful searching in order to be able to find that perfect cat–human bond you've always dreamed of.

What kind of cat is right for you?

Your best match is going to be with a super friendly, cuddly cat who literally can't get enough of people. These types of cats might be a little rarer to come by, but there are plenty around! Registering your interest with your local rehoming centre is certainly a great place to start. If your heart is set on getting a kitten, it will pay to find out a little bit about the personality of the kitten's parents as well as their experiences of being handled to date. Whether you decide to adopt a kitten or obtain one from a breeder, the best kind of kitten for you is going to be one whose parents were also very friendly and tactile with people. Additionally, you'll want to make sure that your kitten has been handled regularly in a positive, gentle manner during his or her sensitive period (2–7 weeks of age). This handling should ideally be done by several different people (preferably four or five) of different ages and characteristics. For this reason, you may want to especially avoid getting older kittens from stray parents because they may be much less likely to have the right combination of factors that you're looking for. If you're keen to obtain a cat from a breeder, be aware that some breeders will be much more responsible and knowledgeable than others.

Simply selecting a certain breed of cat is definitely no guarantee that it will possess the super friendly personality that you're looking for; the personality of the cat's parents and the cat's early handling are going to be much more indicative than just their breed. Additionally, some cat breeds (such as Exotics, Persians, Munchkins and Scottish Folds) can have a range of chronic health problems due to the genetic defects they inherit. Doing some research into which breeds (and breeders) are best to select a cat from is essential. Finally, even though you may love to feel that you are at the centre of your cat's universe, don't forget to also encourage them to still be a cat. You should ideally help them to indulge in a range of other hobbies that don't include human snuggling. A very clingy cat may not be a well-adjusted one, so your cat should also be provided with an exciting, stimulating environment and be encouraged to explore this.

You scored mostly B's and C's – what does this mean?

Your cat parenting aspirations are probably within the average range. You're expecting to be able to hang out regularly with your furry cat pal, although you don't necessarily want to be joined at the hip. This level of flexibility is potentially ideal for cats that are friendly and enjoy the company of humans but also want their own life and not someone hovering over them like a helicopter 24/7. You're likely to find a range of cats that would match well with your style of parenting.

What kind of cat is right for you?

Your best match is going to be a friendly, confident cat who also enjoys going off and doing their own thing. Just like for prospective cat parents scoring mostly A's, you're going to want a cat that's been well-socialised with humans at the right time during their early kittenhood, as well as one that also appears friendly and confident when interacting with you. If you're keen to adopt a cat, your local rehoming centre should be able to help find that perfect feline for you. However, no matter how cute they look, don't be tempted to go for the super active, attention addict or that very petrified-looking stray hiding in the corner. The best way to ensure you have a happy and harmonious cat–human relationship is to go for something in the middle.

You scored mostly D's and E's – what does this mean?

Your approach to cat parenting is probably a bit on the minimalistic side; you're more likely to embrace the part of the cat that speaks to their aloof, independent ancestry. Not all of us necessarily have to fit into the classic cat lover mould, but if we're going to be cat parents, we need to choose the right cat that benefits from this style of parenting. For cats that aren't really into cuddling, if you just provide them with all the physical things that they need and make sure they are in good physical health, this could be more than enough to keep them happy. Not all cats need our love; some may value food and a safe but stimulating place to live a whole lot more. If you're willing to provide these basic things, there may still be the perfect feline out there for you.

What kind of cat is right for you?

Your best match is going to be a cat that's relatively confident or comfortable around people, but also one that doesn't necessarily need much attention from them. You might actually find quite a few of these sorts of cats in rehoming centres. These cats may have been living as pets before and sort of just tolerated it or they may have come in as a stray with no known history. These kinds of cats are likely to need a lot of personal space and alone time. A nice, cat-friendly outdoor space where they can explore to their heart's content is also crucial. Your cat may even prefer to sleep outdoors, so providing a source of shelter and food outside for them may be ideal. If you have a large outdoor area (perhaps you live on a farm or have stables) this might be especially perfect for your independent feline! Be sure that, if you are keen to acquire a cat that doesn't seem to be into cuddles, you don't suddenly change your mind and decide you want some as this is likely to be very stressful for your cat (and potentially also painful for you). Don't forget to make sure any visitors to your house also know what the score is with your self-sufficient fur ball so they don't make the same mistake!

Science corner

What's in a meow? How good are we at understanding our cats when they talk to us?

It's very common for cat owners to have conversations with their cats; the cat meows at us, and we meow (or talk) back to them! However, do we actually know what the cat is trying to tell us? And why do pet cats meow so much?

As kittens, African wildcats, feral domestic cats and pet cats all meow at their mothers. This helps the kitten to communicate when they're cold, in pain or hungry, or if they get trapped or separated from them. However, only pet cats continue to meow a lot as they get older, and this is because we, as owners, encourage this behaviour. Studies have found that the meows made by pet cats actually sound different to those made by feral domestic cats and African wildcats. The meows made by our pets are shorter, higher pitched and sound more pleasant to us. Fascinatingly, pet cats are known to make different types of meows depending on what's going on around them (during feeding time, when stuck somewhere, or when in distress, for example), although each cat may have their own distinctive way of meowing. What studies find is that, in general, people are pretty poor at being able to decipher what these different meows might actually mean (for example, is the cat hungry, do they want attention, or do they need rescuing?). People who like cats, or have more experience with them, tend to do a little better at these tests but the cat's owner may be the best at matching the right meow with the correct scenario. What this research suggests is that cats are certainly trying to communicate with us, but that we probably need a little bit of training from them, in order to understand what it is they actually want from us!

Thank you for reading!

We hope this has been a fun and informative way of learning more about your precious feline, and what makes them tick. Hopefully, you will have discovered something new about their specific character, learnt a little more about their likes and dislikes, and maybe even made some positive changes to improve their lifestyle and wellbeing. To have picked up this book, you no doubt understand how precious the cat–human relationship is, and we hope that the handy tips and tricks in this book will help you and your little one to have an even happier life together.